Praise for *The Sales*

MW01222397

'Highly readable while being challenging and pragmatic. Applying the advice in this excellent book will improve your strategic effectiveness.'
Paul Walsh, CEO, Diageo

'An easy-to-read handbook that will benefit any executive looking to take their business to the next level.'
John Brook, Chairman, Coca-Cola Enterprises

'*The Sales Book* is a thorough guide with surprising and profound advice gathered from the author's many years of practical experience. Good routines and personal integrity are fundamental to long term sales success, and the experienced reader receives a timely reminder of these disciplines.'
Tim Last, Regional Managing Director, Duke Corporate Education

'A great handbook for those interested in starting a career in sales, those needing a checklist to recruit in sales and those in sales management roles. The pitfall so often with seasoned sales people is to think one already knows the basics. This book reminds us that there's always merit in a refresher.'
Agnes Nagy, former sales director for a global packaging company

The Sales Book

The Sales Book

Graham Yemm

PEARSON

Harlow, England • London • New York • Boston • San Francisco • Toronto • Sydney
Auckland • Singapore • Hong Kong • Tokyo • Seoul • Taipei • New Delhi
Cape Town • São Paulo • Mexico City • Madrid • Amsterdam • Munich • Paris • Milan

PEARSON EDUCATION LIMITED
Edinburgh Gate
Harlow CM20 2JE
United Kingdom
Tel: +44 (0)1279 623623
Web: www.pearson.com/uk

First edition published 2013 (print and electronic)

© Pearson Education Limited 2013 (print and electronic)

The right of Graham Yemm to be identified as author of this work has been asserted by him in accordance with the Copyright, Designs and Patents Act 1988.

Pearson Education is not responsible for the content of third-party internet sites.

ISBN: 978-0-273-79291-8 (print)
      978-0-273-79292-5 (PDF)
      978-0-273-79293-2 (ePub)
      978-1-292-00796-0 (eText)

British Library Cataloguing-in-Publication Data
A catalogue record for the print edition is available from the British Library

Library of Congress Cataloging-in-Publication Data
Yemm, Graham.
  The sales book / Graham Yemm.
    pages cm
  Includes index.
  ISBN 978-0-273-79291-8 (pbk.) -- ISBN 987-0-273-79292-5 (PDF) -- ISBN 978-0-273-79293-2 (ePub) -- ISBN 978-1-292-00796-0 (eText)
  1. Selling. 2. Sales management. I. Title.
  HF5438.4.Y46 2013
  658.8'1--dc23
                  2013026017

10 9 8 7 6 5 4 3 2 1
17 16 15 14 13

Cover design by David Carroll & Co
Print edition typeset in 9pt Stone Serif by 3
Print edition printed and bound in Great Britain by Henry Ling Ltd, at the Dorset Press, Dorchester, Dorset

NOTE THAT ANY PAGE CROSS REFERENCES REFER TO THE PRINT EDITION

Contents

About the author

Graham Yemm runs Solutions 4 Training Ltd (*www.solutions 4training.com*). Beginning his career in the corporate world, he moved from sales through to HR, training and into sales management. From here he moved into consultancy, initially as a partner in a successful training consultancy developing and delivering in-house programmes.

Graham is a Fellow of the Institute of Sales and Marketing Management. He has considerable experience in developing and delivering sales programmes and providing consultancy, both in the UK and internationally, for various levels from Sales Directors and Managers through to new sales people.

He has clients in Europe, the Middle East, Russia, Asia and the USA, and he has worked with many different organisations, ranging from petrochemical to pharmaceutical, from financial institutions to computer manufacturers and dealerships, and from telecoms to packaging.

Acknowledgements

I would like to thank all of the colleagues and clients I have worked with over my career. They have helped provide many of the insights which enabled me to write this book.

Publisher's acknowledgements

We are grateful to CSO Insights for permission to use some text on pages 131–2 and the figure on p. 132, © CSO Insights, LLC.

In some instances we have been unable to trace the owners of copyright material, and we would appreciate any information that would enable as to do so.

Introduction

Whether you are starting a new business or involved in a more established one, sales is the essential function. Whatever your product or service you need customers or clients if you are to survive. Without money coming in, the future will be very limited. It is extremely unlikely that you have an offering which is so unique your customers have to come to you. Therefore, you need to be able to generate and achieve sales. You can make the best widgets in the land and have a brilliant marketing team but if you cannot get customers to buy them you will not survive.

This book takes you from the fundamentals of selling, giving an insight into the core skills needed for success, through to providing effective sales direction and leadership. You will understand what is needed to sell effectively and will be able to apply the principles if your role requires you to do so. This will also help if you are responsible for managing others who are selling, or if you need to understand what is required in the sales function. The later chapters focus on the different elements of sales management and direction, helping you to be more confident and capable in these areas. Regardless of your role, there will be something which is relevant and interesting for you.

One of the aims of the book is to cut through many of the misconceptions about selling and the behaviours of sales people. Unfortunately, much of the media attention is directed at various industries which use 'hard' selling tactics and are often very manipulative. For many people this creates a perception about sales and selling which is unfair on the vast majority of companies and sales people who are working hard, with integrity and aiming to do a good job. There are sales techniques which can be learned and applied and fit with the hard sell approach. I make no apology for not endorsing those in this book. The emphasis is towards a relationship or even consultative selling approach, which is being used by the majority of reputable sales forces these days.

There is no single sales model which fits everyone. A number of factors influence what works best for both selling and managing sales. One of the fundamental differences is whether you are in business to business selling (B2B) or business to consumer (B2C). It is possible to be in both, but you need to have specific marketing and sales approaches to address each sector. Although many of the core skills of selling and managing are the same in each sector, there are variations appropriate to each. The content of this book can be taken and applied in either situation; you can decide which ideas and messages are relevant.

Another factor to consider when reading this book is how to adapt your sales approach to fit with the culture. This can be a national or regional culture to your own organisational one. Cultural factors can play a part in which selling style works most effectively. There are times when large organisations have a selling style which they like and believe suits them. It works in some of their markets, especially their home one. Having said that, it does not work in other markets where they operate and their sales management approach is not flexible enough, which costs them business.

Some would argue that many of the principles and ideas covered in this book are out of date and backward looking. There is no place for them in selling in the 21st century. They are entitled to their opinion and there is no doubt technology is playing an ever larger part in sales. Customers use the internet to research suppliers, to price check or even enter e-auctions and post e-tenders. Sales operations research prospective customers on-line, have CRM systems to make planning and reporting easier, and mobile phones, PDAs and other devices make it easier to have information available when out and about. Some are adopting Sales 2.0 tools and social media to be proactive in getting their messages out to prospects. Alongside this, there are a lot of different organisations selling on the internet. This book is not looking at internet selling. It is for organisations that are dealing person to person, even if it is by telephone. They may use technology to support their sales process, but are not using the internet as their primary sales channel. It is good to remember that many people prefer to buy from people.

What you need to succeed in sales

Are sales people born or made? The phrase 'He's a born salesman' can be heard about individuals. What does this mean? Typically, someone who appears to be extrovert, confident and probably who talks positively and enthusiastically (or has the gift of the gab!). If this does not fit you does it mean you cannot be successful in sales? Certainly not. In reality very few successful sales people fit this stereotype: they come in a whole range of shapes, sizes and personalities. If you feel you want to have a career in sales, build sales experience into your career portfolio or you need to incorporate selling with your other work, you can do it.

When considering the requirements for selling successfully a range of factors should be taken into account. The nature of the role is such that you want to make the right choices. Selling can be a very stimulating and satisfying career and, at the same time, it can be challenging and difficult. One of the great things about sales is that it offers a wide selection of options as you develop your experience and build success.

Type of selling

B2B: selling to other businesses. This ranges from Fast Moving Consumer Goods (FMCG), through pharmaceuticals to a variety of industrial or commercial products and services. There is scope to sell highly complex or technical products and solutions through to more simple ones.

B2C: the consumer or end customer is purchasing the product or service. This covers a wide spread of industries, from financial services to home improvements, utilities or telecoms – to name a few.

Unfortunately, the latter is the arena which has tended to attract the poor publicity, and often leads to the dubious reputation of sales as a profession. A number of organisations have used high pressure methods with customers, and in managing their sales people, which has led to a lot of manipulative behaviour. However, these companies constitute a small minority; the vast majority of companies are reputable and professional.

When thinking about choosing between these two there are some fundamental differences to consider (and think how you feel about them). Some general principles are:

B2B	B2C
Usually a larger geographical area to cover.	Probably a more compact, local sales area.
Dealing with organisations and their buying processes and different people.	Dealing directly with the potential customers and users.
Need to understand the customers' business and applications for product or service.	Generally easier to understand how the customers will benefit from product or service.
Likely to have a longer sales lead time.	Likely to have a shorter lead time, or even immediate decisions.

What do you need from yourself?

Like any job, selling needs a combination of the right knowledge, skills and attitudes. These are covered in more detail later in this part. Selling is a function which makes its own special demands on those who do it. Success will depend on a number of factors and these can come from a combination of sources. However, one of the most critical sources is you!

Do some homework to find out about what is really involved in sales roles. What are the challenges faced? These will vary slightly within different markets but many are similar. Ask yourself how ready you are to deal with them. Amongst the most critical requirements will be determination, resilience and motivation. Are you willing and able to keep going when the going gets tough? It might seem clichéd but it is a reality. Can you demonstrate this? You can acquire knowledge about products, market and company. Skills can be learned. It is the personal qualities which can make the difference.

The requirements of sales management

These can be very varied depending on the organisation, the sales structure and the exact responsibilities of the role. Unfortunately, there is often a lack of clarity about the expectations of the job which leads to sales managers struggling to identify and balance their priorities. Within larger organisations there is usually a clearer definition of the roles because there is a sales structure which might span from sales supervisors or area sales managers through divisional sales managers to a sales director. Where this exists it is possible to be more explicit about exactly what is required for each role.

The most fundamental requirement of a sales manager is to be able to manage and lead the sales function effectively so that it delivers the sales target. In order to achieve this the sales manager needs to possess, or be willing to develop, a number of competencies. These would typically include areas such as those shown below. This is not a definitive list and would change according to the particular expectations of an organisation.

Strategic thinking and planning	Sales targeting and forecasting
Understanding of market	Setting sales targets – products, sales territory
Analysis of sales and market information	Anticipating and adapting to market changes
Setting sales strategy – general and for strategic accounts	Accuracy of sales forecasting

Resource planning and organisation

Establishing effective sales structure

Organising internal service and support structure

Recruiting of quality sales people and others

Sales team leadership

Salesforce motivation

Reviewing performance

Skills development of sales team

Field visits and coaching

Personal organisation

Achieving priorities

Time management and organisation

Administration and reporting

Commercial management

Financial awareness and understanding

Setting and working to budgets

Using financial and commercial information

Sales direction and control

Setting sales activities and objectives

Using CRM or reporting system

Monitoring performance and taking action

Interactions with other departments

Relationships with colleagues

Understanding of roles and objectives

Keeping other functions informed

Communication

Communicating with sales team

Presentation skills

Relationships with customers

Approachable – listener

General management skills

Managing and leading change

Problem solving

Decision making

If sales management appeals to you, think about how these fit with your understanding of the role. Whether you are thinking of moving into sales management or are already in it, evaluate your level of capability against each and identify the key areas for improvement.

The later stages of the book cover the main elements of the sales manager and sales director roles. It is important to recognise that the essential route to success is through recruiting the right sales people for your market, providing them with clear direction, ongoing support and development so that they are motivated and able to perform consistently. In time they will become even better and produce even more. It sounds easy when written like that, but it is an ongoing challenge. As the sales manager you need to remember that your sales target and growth will come through improvements from your sales people – not from you doing more selling.

Fundamentals for selling

What is selling and what type is right for the organisation?

Objectives

- To help you understand what is selling and a key phrase to remember throughout your sales career
- To explain the different types of sales approach
- To enable you to recognise which is the most effective approach for your market

Understanding

When building a house, or any structure, a key for creating a stable product is to make sure the foundations are suitable. With successful selling the same principles apply. Too many people either enter sales or are involved in it without having a real understanding of the fundamentals.

I had been involved with sales in various roles for about 10 years without really considering them. It was only when a participant on a training course I was running asked the presenter, 'How can I be expected to sell if I can't cut my prices?' What was really concerning was that the participant had been selling on the road for the company for about eighteen months and on their inside sales desk for a year! The on-going conversation made me realise that I had never stopped to think about some of the real basics. I had joined a company which provided a good sales training programme combined with regular field sales management and support. I just followed what they told me to do and it produced results so I never stopped to look for deeper understanding. However, this incident in the training course made me think again. I decided to start all future programmes differently.

The first basic step is to address something which I believe is very misunderstood: understanding what is selling. The dictionary I used provided two parts to its definition.

To sell: 'To exchange products or services for money or kind. *To convince of value.*'

The first part seems obvious, but it is the second which I would encourage you to remember and apply in your sales role. Who defines value and decides if something offers or gives value? It is not the seller, nor the marketing department. The skilled sales person will develop a good relationship with the prospect so that they will be comfortable to talk about what they are looking for in terms of value.

Salesmanship: 'To present products or wares in an attractive light. *To persuade or influence purchasers to buy.*'

Again, the key part of the definition is the second. It is not just a play on words. If someone believes they have bought something it is 180° from feeling they have been sold it. (There is less chance of 'buyer's remorse'!)

These definitions are valid in any sort of selling and especially those with direct person to person contact. The actual monetary worth of a sale, whether £10, £100 or £1000 or more, is not a factor. As Peter Drucker said in *The Practice of Management* (1954): 'The only purpose of a business is to create and keep a customer.' This requires good selling and service.

The market influences the most effective choice of sales strategy and sales approach. There are four types of sales approach.

Transactional selling: *The one-off sale. The focus is on winning the order.* This is probably what most people think of when they hear about sales people and selling. There are many, very good, reputable organisations which use this sales approach and a large number of professional sales people work for them. However, it is the area where most of the misconceptions about selling arise and much of the media attention on dubious sales techniques is focused.

There are specific challenges with this approach. The sellers need a lot of possible contacts coming in to the top of the sales funnel and they have to keep on coming. There is no real repeat business to build upon. If selling in this arena you need to be able to take the constant change of contacts and transitory relationships, because as you close each order you have to move on to finding the next one. This type of sales approach can be used for a number of sectors, such as double-glazing, one-off items such as photocopiers or even office furniture. There may be scope for small, additional sales to customers, but the primary sale is the first one.

Relationship selling: *The ongoing sale with repeat business. The focus is on the relationship.* Many markets lend themselves to this approach. You need to recognise that you start more slowly and be patient, often building from smaller orders on to larger ones as the relationship develops. There will probably be a longer sales cycle and managing the sales people and overall operation requires a more flexible monitoring system.

A useful way to consider customers when using this approach is to think about their CLV (Customer Lifetime Value.) Think about how long they typically stay with you, or could, and what is their average purchase value. Multiply the two elements and see what you arrive at. The number might be surprising. For example, a small local printer might change their attitudes towards customers if they calculated their overall expenditure. Imagine, they have a number of small customers who order once a month and spend £50 each time. They would use the printer for four years. Their CLV is £50 × 12 months × 4 years = £2,400. Does the printer start to think of them as more important now?

Relationship selling is relevant in many markets including areas such as distributors or wholesalers, products being used in an ongoing manner (whether packaging materials or professional services).

Consultative selling: *Getting even closer to the customer to understand them and their issues. The focus is on solutions and not* *products.* This type of selling is becoming more recognised, although many would claim it is not anything new and is what good sales people have been doing for years. It is not right for every market, organisation or sales person. If you are involved in this type of selling it provides its own challenges for you and your sales management. It might be seen as more low-key because there needs to be more emphasis on the questioning and exploration of the prospect's situation and challenges. It is sometimes tricky to resist the temptation to talk about your products or services and to keep the focus on the customer and their issues.

In some respects, consultative selling can be used in a number of relationship selling areas as well as where dealing with higher value contract or complex sales solutions. This might include information technology, industrial sales with involved production processes or where your product or service will have a significant impact on their business.

Partnership selling: *Combines the principles of consultative selling with account management.* A balanced approach, this is particularly effective if you have any sort of key account management strategy. Although this might be your aim, it is much more productive if the customer wants to work this way with you. This does require a broader skill set to use it well and an awareness of how to balance your priorities.

This is not industry or sector specific but is likely to be effective with business to business markets. It will apply when your organisation has recognised that it wants to move into a key or strategic account management strategy for the target accounts which fit its target criteria.

Doing

Remember that good selling is about helping people to buy. It is much easier to get and keep customers this way. It is not about pushing your product or service. Build the relationship to develop trust with the prospect.

Ask questions and listen carefully to the answers and you can find out what they consider to be value. Always remember, it is their definition of value, not yours or your marketing people's, which matters. Value is personal, subjective and might be illogical, irrational and changeable. Part of the fun in selling is establishing this trust and understanding someone's idea of value. No two sales visits are exactly the same. Concentrate on showing prospects how you can help them meet their value criteria from within your organisation. The better you become, the more people will want to buy from you.

Understand the type of selling which is appropriate for your organisation in relation to the target market. Be clear about the differences between them and develop the right skills for that approach.

The sales person's checklist

- Concentrate on getting prospects to talk more than you in your sales calls. Think about how you can get them to do this.

- Remember 'telling is not selling'. Practise developing your listening in all areas of life: with friends, family, colleagues – and customers.

- Good selling is about helping people to buy. Identify ways in which you can encourage prospects to open up to you and tell you what they consider to be value.

- For any type of selling apart from transactional, consider calculating the CLV for each customer. When you are approaching prospective customers it can be helpful to think about what they can be worth over time.

Knowledge, skills and attitudes for success

Objectives

- To understand the key items under each of the categories of knowledge, skills and attitudes for sales success in the relevant sales approach
- To use the items listed to identify how well you fit with the requirements
- To identify your strengths for the role
- To recognise the areas where you can improve or develop

Understanding

Every job requires a combination of factors and sales is no exception. There is no single success formula for sales. A wide range of personality types, physical characteristics, education levels and career backgrounds can be found across sales forces and amongst top performers. What they will have in common is a significant number of the characteristics shown in the table below under the three categories, knowledge, skills and attitudes.

Some industries or markets require their sales people to have certain educational qualifications because technical issues or product complexity make it easier for the sellers to pick up the knowledge and understanding more easily. It could also help with customer meetings, establishing credibility and building trust. However, this does not apply with many other markets. If someone has the willingness and determination and possesses the right attitudes they can become successful sellers. (I do not fit most of the 'typical' profiles of sales people, nor the perception of what type of person goes into sales. When I went into selling I was naturally shy, not particularly confident or outgoing. Over the years, I have not done badly in sales and I am still fundamentally the same person as I was when I started.)

The different types of selling outlined in the previous chapter have a number of common elements in each category plus their own more specialised requirements. The following table has a list of suggestions for each of the categories with specific ideas for the more focused sales approaches.

Knowledge	Skills	Attitudes
General		
Product – application	Planning	Positive
Customer – structure, their business	Communication	Confident
	Questioning	Listening
Own company – structure, capability and limitations	Presentation	Resilient
	Benefit selling	Empathy
Market – which sector you are selling into	Objection handling	Determination
	Closing	Flexibility
Competition		Perseverance
Territory – sales area		
Relationship selling		
Customer's structure	Interpersonal	Patience
	Administrative	Proactive
	Customer management	Open-minded
	Relationship building	
	Negotiation	
Consultative selling		
Customer's business	Research	Curiosity
Customer's market	Preparation	Self-confidence
Market trends	Questioning in depth	Creative
Competition – strengths and weaknesses	Spotting opportunities	Solution oriented
	Developing solutions	
Commercial elements of customer's business	Influencing	
	Presenting solutions	

Knowledge	Skills	Attitudes
Partnership selling		
Customer's strategy	Team working	Willingness to trust in others
Company strategy	Co-ordination	
Company capability and limitations	Organisation	Open to ideas from others
	Multi-tasking	
Contact base in customer	Balancing short-, medium- and long-term thinking	
Financial awareness		
	Handling complexity	
	Decision making	
	Diplomacy	

You may be able to identify additional items you want to add to each of the categories. However, the list gives an indication of what is required for success. Knowledge can be acquired over time and found from a range of sources. You should take responsibility for developing your knowledge in each area and keeping it up to date. Skills are developed through training, coaching and practise. In my experience a weakness for many sales people is that they are reluctant to recognise their own skill gaps or to accept that they need to keep practising and improving them. The attitudes come from within. Although a seller does not need to have all of these, it helps if the majority are present and the individual is willing to realise that these are important and accesses them more.

Doing

If you are reading this with a view to going into sales you can use the list to consider whether selling is right for you. If you are already in it you can think about what to do to improve your own performance, or what areas you need to develop. If you are responsible for recruiting and managing sales people, it can give you a good basis for assessment when interviewing or leading them.

It might be of help if you understand the 'Conscious Competence Learning Model'. (No one knows for certain who created this, although it is often attributed to Noel Burch when he was at Gordon Training International.)

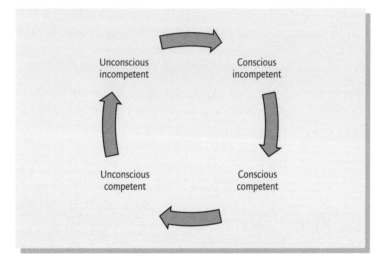

Think about something like learning to drive, to play a musical instrument or a sport. How did you go through this cycle?

Conscious incompetent: You know you do not know something, you are aware of your limited skills or knowledge. You start to learn whatever it is, possibly using a variety of methods.

Conscious competent: You now have a reasonable grasp of the basics and continue to improve and develop your ability mainly through 'doing' and practising. However, you still have to think about what you are doing and check whether it is right. You are not fully confident at this stage.

Unconscious competent: You reach the level where you can do things without needing to think about the detail of the method or process. You do the fundamentals automatically and feel confident and comfortable with what you are doing.

Unconscious incompetent: This has two levels. The first is before you undertake something where you do not know what you do not know. The second, and more worrying, is the stage that happens after you are an 'unconscious competent'. This occurs because you stop thinking about what you are doing and, if you are not careful, bad habits creep in. If these are not identified and corrected they can become more and more ingrained and performance will decline. (What happens with your driving if you have a near miss, or see a bad accident? Most of us move back to conscious competent and then forward again. We pay attention to what we are doing and concentrate more for a while.)

When starting out in sales you are likely to be at 'conscious incompetent' and with time you move on to 'conscious competence'. At these stages you will be more aware of areas where you can develop and more open to accepting ideas for improving yourself. You begin to apply this alongside your natural skills and attitudes, and with more selling experience you move to 'unconscious competent' where you are applying these more confidently and fluently. You get better sales results more consistently. However, this can be the danger time! There is a risk you can become complacent and bad habits will creep into how you work. To be a real professional, make sure you check where you are in this cycle, both as a whole and for specific elements of your job. If you are working in an organisation where you have sales management support, use it to help to keep you moving between 'unconscious competent' and 'conscious competent'.

Take some time to look back to the table, starting from the beginning and working through to whatever type of selling you think you will be doing. Use it to do a self-assessment against each item and first identify your strengths. Which items do you recognise you can improve? Consider where you are in the conscious competence cycle and what you can do to move onward with it.

Look at the knowledge category first. When thinking about the items ask yourself how well you could describe each to someone else? It is a useful test for how good your knowledge is and helps you to identify the specific areas where you can improve. Once you have done this, consider how you can acquire the level of knowledge you feel is needed. How much can you do for yourself? There are many options, such as researching on the internet, reading other material, talking to colleagues and customers to name a few. To a great extent your own curiosity will be a key driver in this.

When you move on to the skills category do the same and identify those items where you feel you are strong. (This does not mean you cannot improve and develop these!) Be honest about the ones where you have scope to be better. Knowing your skill levels are good or even excellent can do wonders for your confidence. Take care to avoid becoming complacent. We are all at risk from skills erosion, especially those who rarely stop to assess their performance or do not have the benefit of any coaching.

The attitudes category is different to the other two because these have to come from within. You either need to have these already and be using them in the way you behave or to recognise that you need to have them and start to build them. You can develop many of these attitudes when you have identified them and decided to think and act accordingly. It will take time for them to grow and become part of your behavioural style. Putting it simply, your attitudes will underpin how well you use the skills you are developing and how you apply the knowledge you have.

The sales person's checklist

- Take responsibility for your own development. If your organisation has the capability of offering support and training, be proactive in asking for it. If this is not available, look for other options for getting what you need.

- Keep yourself out of 'unconscious incompetence'. Carry out your self-assessment against each of the items on the table every three months.

- Set yourself goals for specific levels of knowledge in the different areas. Keep working at each area because things are always changing and you need your knowledge to be current. It helps your confidence and your credibility.

■ Identify the key skills you want to develop and plan how to acquire them. (Training courses, on-line programmes, reading, observing others, coaching are some of the options.)

■ Ask for feedback and suggestions for your own development. Use colleagues, friends and even customers!

Managing time effectively

Objectives

- To understand how to establish priorities for your activities
- To plan to use your time more effectively
- To appreciate why it pays to make time for planning

Understanding

Time is something we often undervalue and do not think about as a resource. We actually take it for granted and forget it is the ultimate perishable resource. When that hour has gone it cannot be regained or replaced. I admit that I had this approach to how I spent my time until moving into the world of consultancy where the main commodity I had available to sell was my time. Once I was charging based on time it suddenly had a real value. It also made me consider the worth of my time when doing other parts of the job and even my own personal time.

Within a sales role, time is an important element to consider for many reasons. Depending on the country you are working in, and the business culture, you will have around 200–220 selling days available each year. Your own organisational structure and your role might mean that you have significantly fewer days than this. Making the best use of your time is vital.

What stops you using your time effectively? There is probably a combination of factors, starting with not understanding how to do so. Many people involved with selling are too reactive and think that being busy is more important rather than whether they are effective. It is a natural tendency to spend time on the parts of the job which you enjoy or feel comfortable with and to want to respond to events. The question is whether acting this way is dealing with the activities which contribute to your results?

Some years ago I heard the idea that a sales person's time could be split into three areas.

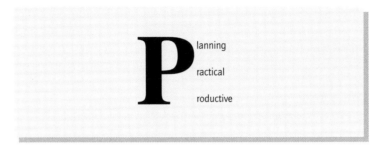

Planning
ractical
roductive

Planning time: This can range from looking at your overall target market, through territory management and journey planning to preparation for specific calls.

Practical time: The practicalities of doing the job fall into this heading. These include travelling, waiting for appointments, writing proposals and dealing with your general administration.

Productive time: The critical part of time use, where you are in contact with a decision maker or someone within the Decision Making Unit (DMU). This might be actual face-to-face meetings, web-Ex, telephone calls or any other direct contact.

When looking at most sales operations, the way these Ps are split tends to be with the smallest proportion on planning; by far the largest proportion is practical, and productive time is in the middle, but usually towards the lower end. Logic suggests that increasing the amount of productive time is likely to improve sales results. What has to change to achieve this? The simple equation is to invest more time in 'planning' in order to reduce 'practical' time and increase 'productive' time. This might seem obvious, but many people, not just in sales, do not appreciate the value of planning and do not devote enough time to it.

Doing

Identify the key activities required to do your job effectively. These could range from researching the market and prospects, through planning your week and month, to preparing for sales calls, telephone and e-mail contact, sales meetings to writing proposals and following up on them – and anything else specific for your role. When you have listed these, think about prioritising them. Whether you give them an A (*must do*), B (*ought to do*), C (*nice to do, will do*) or put them into the figure below does not matter. It is recognising the need to do the exercise and actually carrying it out that is important.

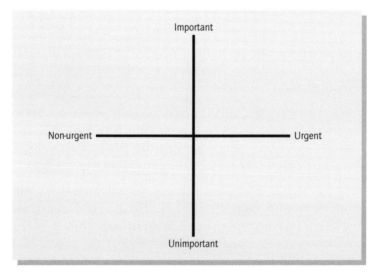

Take an honest look at yourself and how you use your time at the moment. Be willing to identify the bad habits which creep in and the time stealers which might distract you from the core activities of your job. It can help to write these down so that you really see what they are. Now think about what you can do to reduce or remove these to free you up to focus on using your time more positively and constructively.

Start to develop good time habits. Use a diary system, electronic or manual, which suits you. Have a monthly plan and overview for setting appointments, follow-up calls and planning for your 'A' priority or 'Important/Non-urgent' activities. Begin to use a weekly or daily plan (or 'to do list') depending on your preference. Stick with these for a month so that they become a habit. Having these will help you to keep your focus and not get too distracted. Make sure you are planning time in sensible blocks, rather than chopping and changing activities. It will prove far more efficient and effective.

An important consideration is that you will be able to recognise when something has taken you away from your planned activities and know what you need to return to doing. You will also be able to deal with a number of time stealers more positively and feel more confident about not getting caught up with them.

The sales person's checklist

- Beware the risk of thinking you know how your time is being used. Keep a time log of your activities for a week to see how you really spend your time, not how you think you do.

- Set some targets to increase your 'productive' time, including e-mail, telephone and face-to-face time.

- List your key activities and prioritise them. A good idea is to have these written out and put somewhere where you will regularly see them so that you keep them in mind.

- Begin using monthly planners and weekly or daily ones. Find a system or method which you are comfortable with: there are no 'right' ones!

- Check your time use every month and assess how you have spent it across the three Ps.

The first steps – finding potential customers

Objectives

- To recognise the importance of identifying potential 'suspects'
- To understand the difference between a suspect and a prospect
- To recognise what sort of factors to consider when qualifying prospects
- To identify how to check whether a suspect can become a prospect

Understanding

A common concept in sales is that of the 'funnel' or 'pipeline'. The principle is that there is a process or flow which requires potential sales opportunities at the beginning and after various stages it leads to some of these becoming customers. There are differing views about the exact structure or composition of the funnel and what might be included. Another variable is the content and stages which are appropriate for your market. However, one thing they will have in common is that they start with needing to have a number of possible customers. At this stage, they are typically referred to as 'suspects'. They will be people or organisations which *might* buy from you.

The next step in the sales funnel or pipeline is to identify which of them can be become 'prospects'. These are extremely important in the sales process. Rather than people who might have a want or need for what you are offering, the prospect has a want or need and is likely to buy. The issue is whether they purchase it from you or someone else. A key point to understand is that not all suspects become prospects for a variety of reasons, many of which are outside your control or influence. However, as you develop your selling skills you will probably get better at identifying suspects and turning them into qualified prospects.

Many sales people have an expectation that their company should provide a constant supply of suspects. In an ideal world this would be the case. However, it is not always feasible because of budget or resource constraints. Too often, sales people are eager to find an excuse for their own struggles and it is easy to point the finger at the company or marketing. Yes, it is good if they can provide some leads or suspects but not necessarily all of them. These days, it is possible to get a wide range of data in the form of various lists of possible contacts. A few of these might be good value and can help to provide a focus of activity. This is especially true if you are selling relatively high value products or services to clearly defined markets. The investment in the potential target customer base can help the sales people to be more effective in their activities if it is accurate.

The essential step is to check whether the suspect is a prospect, or has the potential to become one. This is important so that you do not spend too much time pursuing lost causes! Remember, time is a limited resource you need to use wisely. Again, different organisations and sales people will have variations in their definitions of a prospect. There is not one answer to fit all companies. The term is short for a prospective customer. This can give you a clue about how you can qualify prospects. How would you know they are more likely to buy than other suspects?

Identifying a list of criteria will help you assess whether someone, or an organisation, qualifies as a prospect. These criteria might include some fundamental factors such as having a budget to spend, authority to spend it, and possibly looking to purchase within a specific timescale. Decide on the levels you need for each with the option of adding a further rating to think about where they might fit on a scale from lukewarm through to hot. The ideal for any seller is to have a number of 'hot prospects' because they are the ones who are going to make a buying decision in the very near future.

A good measure of your development, and effectiveness, is to assess the ratio between the number of suspects contacted and the number of qualified prospects you can identify. As this improves it indicates that you are getting better at targeting suspects. You can then look at how many prospects become customers and keep a note of what progress you make with this ratio.

Doing

Identifying possible suspects can be done using a number of methods. Your sales approach will influence which of these work best for your organisation.

- Researching companies, using the internet, can be a good starting point.
- Using a well-defined or targeted list (usually from a third party provider).
- Checking professional or trade bodies to see if you can get lists of members is another option.
- Reading industry magazines or blogs, local or national press can provide both names and information. Do look at the recruitment sections too, to see what positions might have a new person in them in the near future.
- Networking can be beneficial, provided you have identified the right groups. Apart from attending meetings there might be opportunities to speak or present at these or for local branches of trade bodies.
- Use social media and networks such as LinkedIn (especially for B2B sales).
- Asking for referrals is effective, although many sales people are reluctant to ask their contacts if they know of anyone else who might be interested in their product.
- Use technology to help. Many more suspects are open to

early approaches and interactions via e-mail and similar contact. It can be time efficient for both parties.

- Last, but not least, can be pure prospecting either by telephone or calling at the customer's premises.

Running through all of these is having some sort of customer record system or database to record names, contact details, status and actions. Whether this is a full CRM system, a simpler sales contact management system or a basic database depends on your company and the sales operation. The important thing is, whatever the system, it has to be used to have any value.

Make time to carry out the activities suggested above and aim to identify and make a specific number of contacts every week or month. Do be realistic and accept that not everyone will welcome your approach with open arms. There is some evidence that too many sales people give up too early in their efforts to get to meet suspects. Those who persist for five attempts or more have a better chance of success.

When approaching suspects understand what qualifies them as a genuine prospect. This will help you make better use of your time, and qualifying out those who are not prospects is just as important as establishing those who are. Many sales people are not rigorous enough in doing this and expend too much effort in trying to convert suspects who are not ready nor able to be potential customers now or in the short or medium term.

What specific criteria will define a qualified prospect for your marketplace? There may be some differences for first-time users of your product or service compared with prospects who are currently buying from a competitor.

- Did they approach you?
- Check if they have a budget to spend on your product. Is it available now or at some time in the future? What is it?
- Can they place the order or authorise the expenditure?
- Who else might be involved in the decision process?
- When do they want to have the product or service in place?

- Do they have to place an order with someone?
- If they are using a competitor, is there a contract? When is it due for renewal?
- Are they open to considering another supplier?

Make sure you keep a record of any potential prospects, including the answers to the qualifying criteria. Not everyone will be a hot prospect, but you need to keep in touch with those who might be in the medium term. Over time you can build the relationship and also their urgency might increase and they become warmer and warmer.

Remember, not every prospect will become a customer. Your prospects will almost certainly be targeted by your competitors and they may win the business. This does not mean you give up. Maintain a good relationship with all prospects because you may be able to turn them into customers at a later date. Circumstances change, competitors do not always get it right and prospects might be happy to use you in the future if you make it easy for them.

The sales person's checklist

- Identify the key elements of your pipeline or sales funnel. Work out how many 'suspects' you need to identify each week or month.

- Where can you find the possible 'suspects' for your product or service? Use a range of resources to widen your spread of opportunity – unless you are in a very niche market.

- Set yourself a target for how many 'suspects' you will contact each week or month. Input too few at the start of the pipeline process and you will have too few sales emerging at the other end.

- Adopt a 'one out – one in' approach. When someone either orders or drops out of the process for whatever reason, replace

them with another suspect. Keep your level consistent to
maintain the flow.

- Identifying prospects is vital and it needs to be done effectively.
Do not guess or hope! Develop your own list of qualification
criteria and questions.

- Information is important for professional selling. Set up a
record system, or learn how to use the one in your organisation
if it already exists.

- Work out the ratios from suspects → prospects → customers
and monitor them from month to month. Know whether you
are on track and make adjustments if you slip.

- If a prospect does not buy from you now, they do not
necessarily drop right off your radar. Use the follow-up process
so that you can act when they might be in the market in the
future.

Why people buy

Objectives

- To understand the concept of needs and wants
- To be able to identify the difference between implicit and explicit needs and why they matter in selling
- To know how to establish prospects' 'shopping lists' which equal their idea of value
- To identify the different ways people arrive at the point where they are convinced

Understanding

When we believe we are getting value we go ahead and buy whatever product or service we are looking at. There is not a magic formula for finding this out, because every one of us has our own, subjective definition of value. Occasionally, prospects can be 'sold' something using the more pushy sales techniques where the seller has been able to trigger some of the buying motives of the prospect. If you are selling in a market where you want to generate repeat business it is preferable your customers feel as though they are buying from you. They will be more likely to come back. By understanding how prospects arrive at their point of making a buying decision you can make your own life easier. Sell to them in a way they want to buy.

Whether selling to organisations, individuals or families, the prospects will have some key similarities with regard to how they arrive at their decision to buy. They will have a combination of logical and emotional criteria which have to be met, usually referred to as needs and wants. For example, if you are thinking of buying a watch, why do you need one? If it is to have something to help you know the time that is the need. Which make and model do you choose? A Rolex is not bought as a need purchase, nor are many makes. This could be driven by the brand name and status, the appearance and style or just a feel-good element. They are the want. A widely stated view is that people buy on emotion but justify their decisions rationally. Many Rolex purchasers will have ways to justify why they chose their watch. There are various arguments about the split between emotion and logic in final decision. Whichever you read, they all make the point that emotion is the larger part. This is one of the reasons why the relationship and rapport building is so essential because that is the initial emotional stage which the prospect goes through before buying anything.

You can test this out for yourself. Think about a recent purchase you have made that you consider a reasonably major one. (Not a day-to-day, or regular item for now.) List your reasons for choosing the particular product or service and, when you have done this, do the same for why you used the supplier you bought it from. Now split out the criteria between those which are logical and those which are emotive. If you are honest with yourself you will find that the emotive list is longer.

There are many levels of emotional need. The most fundamental way of thinking about these is the consideration of whether someone is buying to avoid pain or for gain or pleasure. Although it might be surprising, many buying decisions are made to avoid pain. (Not necessarily physical pain, but actual or potential 'pain' or problems either with the present situation or what might happen if they do nothing.) Whether in organisational purchasing or personal, many people prefer to keep the status quo rather than change, unless there is a compelling reason. Bear this in mind before you spend too long stressing the gains from choosing your product or service; they may not be relevant to the prospect if they want to avoid pain. These will be the fundamental triggers to prompt the buying decision. We then add the other criteria as our 'shopping list'. When we can tick off the items on our list we feel we are getting value.

As you move forward with your selling skills you will become better at understanding the different levels of need which prospects have.

Latent: These are hidden, frequently because the prospect is unaware of the need and feels content with the current state. This situation may appear to hold little opportunity for a sale, however the reverse may be true. A good, aware seller may be able to bring this need to the surface with the right questioning, moving it through the following stages.

Implied: The prospect has a sense that something could change or improve, but is unclear about how to bring it about. This need is often expressed as a degree of dissatisfaction with the present situation or talking about a problem or irritation. You can influence the prospect by questioning and being a sounding board about the present and desired situations. This can then make the need move to the next type, below.

Explicit: When the prospect is clear about the gap between their current and desired situation. They usually make direct statements about what they want or need to have.

Doing

Once you have developed the right level of rapport and established the relationship it is time to start to explore the needs. Using the questioning skills from the previous chapter is key to this. My suggestion is that you begin this step by establishing the prospect's 'shopping list'. You may need to do this more than once if you are meeting different people within the DMU, because each person will have their own set of criteria. Choose some questions which you feel comfortable with. The type of question could be:

- 'When choosing a supplier of ..., what is important to you?'
- 'When you made your last purchasing decision, what made you choose that supplier?'
- 'What factors (or criteria) do you look for from suppliers you use?'

Once finished, keep quiet and give the prospect time to think about their response. They may need this because they have not been asked before nor do they have the answers on the tip of their tongue. Depending on what you are selling and whether it is possible, the next tip is to write down their answers using their words. As you write their responses you will probably get comments such as 'quality', 'service', 'reliability' and similar words or phrases. Do this so that they can see what you are doing if they choose to look. There are several reasons for doing this. The first is to let them know you are paying attention to what they are saying. The second is to give you thinking time. The third is to remind you to avoid the classic sales mistake – assuming. You have to avoid making an ASS of U and ME. If the prospect has told you that one of their shopping list criteria is 'service', what do you think it means? Bad news, your answer is irrelevant. Especially as it might be a different answer to the prospect's idea of service. Read through the items you have listed and any which might be at all ambiguous, qualify. Just ask them: 'Exactly what do you mean by service, just so I can really understand what you are looking for?' Again, write down their response.

When you have their 'shopping list' you know the major part of what they feel is value. You will need to direct your sales presentation towards these criteria and not to other elements which are absent from their list. They will not add value.

The next part is to begin to check the specific needs and make them explicit. Sometimes it is made easier for you when the prospect tells you about some explicit needs (e.g. 'We need help with reducing our energy costs'). Even when you have identified the wants and needs you are only part of the way to the sale. People will be convinced, or convince themselves, in different ways. Some need to see the product or service in use, some like to read about it and have information to study and others need to experience, feel or try it. You can check which of these might apply to your prospect by asking them, 'How do you know when you have made the right purchasing decision?' Their answer will indicate which option they prefer.

The sales person's checklist

■ Carry out the 'shopping list' exercise for yourself, identifying product or service and suppliers. To really understand the principle, ask several friends to do the same and note their lists. Differentiate the emotive and logical factors.

■ Develop two or three questions to help you ask prospects for their 'shopping lists'. Keep testing and using them until you have the ones which feel right for you.

■ Start to write prospects' responses and always qualify any which might be ambiguous. Do not ASS-U-ME!

■ List some examples of possible explicit needs which your prospects might have or state. Learn these so that you can spot them. Keep adding to your list as you hear new ones.

■ Test out how people make their buying decisions by asking friends and colleagues how they know they have made the right decision. Then ask about how many times they need to see/hear/feel/try.

part

two

Starting the sale

Pre-call preparation

Objectives

- To understand why thorough preparation is essential and a key priority activity
- To know what elements to cover in your pre-call preparation
- To be able to approach your calls with confidence

Understanding

Preparation is key to making successful sales calls, whether on the telephone or face to face, initial calls or ongoing calls. Too many people moving into sales think that they can succeed through good interpersonal skills or by using their own personality without bothering to spend time preparing. They may get occasional results, but are unlikely to get consistent success. It is too easy to find excuses for not doing the necessary preparation. They do not see time doing the preparation as contributing towards achieving their target. They suffer from 'busyness' without thinking about whether they are actually being effective. Neglecting this stage can lead to any one of a range of pitfalls such as seeing unqualified prospects, not considering the other person's possible objectives, not being flexible in approach and, ultimately, lost opportunities and wasted time.

If you want to be in a stronger position to achieve your target and to feel in more control of your sales performance, recognise that investing time in preparation is as valuable as meeting prospects and customers. It has a direct influence on your confidence and approach to prospects. There are five distinct areas to consider in your preparation:

1 The prospect you are going to call or visit – e.g. who they are, their position, information about their organisation, what is happening in their market or business?

2 The purpose of the call – what do you want to achieve?

3 Their objectives – what might they want to get from the meeting?

4 The support material you need – e.g. product information, literature, customer references.

5 Yourself – e.g. attitude, frame of mind, appearance.

Making time for this is part of the Planning P, in Part one. Put blocks of time throughout your week to address the overall preparation and then check the specifics each day when considering each call. This is an activity which needs to have a high priority and not be thought of as an optional extra.

Your overall planning and preparation will be helped if you have a good record or CRM system. This does depend on how well you use it, both in updating the system and analysing what information it contains. If you have started to complete the records from the 'suspect' stage, you have something to build upon. The amount of information and detail will vary depending on the market you are selling in but, in principle, the more you have the better. Once you have had initial contact the record system starts to come into its own. Rather than hope to remember details in your head, put them into the system and let it do the memorising for you! Before your next contact, refer to the system and bring back the details of the person, their situation, any objectives and actions from the previous call. From this, you have the basis for your pre-call preparation.

Doing

When starting work on your pre-call preparation, whatever market you are selling on, or whether by phone or face to face, find out what works best for you. The ideas suggested here can be moved around in the order in which you do them. The important thing is to cover them!

The first step is to assess 'Where are we now?' by using your records and any other sources of information to carry out a basic situational analysis. Answer these:

- Who am I due to see?
- What is their relationship with me? With my organisation?
- What is happening in their market? What are their competitors doing?
- Who initiated the contact?
- Who else do they deal with in our market?
- What is their budget? Other financial factors?
- What is their timescale?
- What do I want to achieve from the call? (This could include building the relationship, getting information, an order, or resolving a query or problem.)
- What might they want to achieve from the call? (This could be similar to your list.)

Think about any other questions you would add to your own checklist.

When you are comfortable with your answers to these questions think about what you need to have to hand to help you in the call.

- What company brochures or information can I use?
- Do I have the appropriate samples or examples (if relevant)?
- What product data or technical information is available?
- Do I have examples I can use based on other customers using my product or service? (These might be written up as case studies or more anecdotal.)
- Are there customers who I can quote as reference sites?
- What about market data, reports or press comments?
- If using a laptop or tablet, have any relevant information saved into a folder for easy access during the call.
- Have the customer's file open for easy viewing.

Your record system will support you with all of this and is part of a simple process when used effectively.

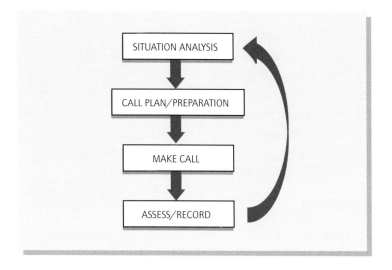

The third phase is to look at yourself.

- Do you enough have business cards?
- Are you familiar with the samples (or examples) and comfortable demonstrating them?
- Have you double-checked the questions and what you need to take?
- What dress code will be fitting with the prospect? (E.g. if you are selling to farmers, you do not wear a suit – they will think you are from the bank or the tax authorities!)
- Are you in the right frame of mind for making the call? Feeling confident because you have done the preparation? If you have had a couple of knock-backs in the day, put them behind you and think about the next call going well.
- Double-check appearance (for face-to-face calls) and think about having a mint or similar beforehand, especially if you have been eating garlic or spicy food.

The final step takes place just before the call. Take a few minutes to look back over what you have covered, double-check your information and your initial plan and organise yourself. This is essential for your creating a good first impression.

The sales person's checklist

- Recognise that making time for planning and preparation is a key priority for effective and professional selling. Block time to do it and avoid trying to fit it in as an afterthought.

- Your record system is your friend provided you use it effectively. (If your organisation does not have a system, develop one or search for what is available. There is a wide choice and you will be able to find something suitable.)

- Share ideas with colleagues where you can, or friends if operating on your own. Ask them how they approach their preparation. Getting ideas from others can help you build on your own.

- Preparation will reduce the risk of poor calls or inefficient visits, but it does not promise to work every time. Develop your own checklists for 'where you are now', 'where you want to be', 'what you need to take and do', and 'what you need to check for yourself'.

- Review calls to assess how they went compared with your plan. Where there are any gaps, think about why they occurred and what you can do to stop this happening in future calls. Whilst doing this, check whether there are any patterns to the gaps.

- It takes time to create good habits. Stick with your blocks of time, using your checklists and record system for at least three to four weeks. (Remember, you will take time to become 'consciously competent' before moving to the 'unconscious competent' stage.)

Who to talk to

Objectives

- To understand the concept of the Decision Making Unit
- To recognise the need to develop your range of contacts within prospective customers
- To understand the different types of buyer or influencer within the Decision Making Unit

Understanding

Buying decisions are rarely, if ever, made by one individual without any influence from others, even for people who are buying something personally. This influence might be from the media, websites, friends, family. Within organisations it could be through formal reporting lines or job roles, or colleagues who have an involvement with the eventual decision.

Different sales development and training companies have created their own labels to define the various roles involved within the decisions process. Within most organisational purchasing processes there are several 'typical' roles which are involved. Having said this, several of the roles might be held by one person and, conversely, there might be more than one person for each role. Whatever the labels, the decision maker will have others around, somewhat like the diagram below (where D.M. = a decision maker, D.I. = a decision influencer).

Many sales people are aware of the principle of building a relationship with the decision maker. However, actually identifying who this is and how to get to talk or meet with them is not always easy. This is not an excuse for giving up. If you find this key person difficult to reach, it is probable that your competitors do too. Perseverance pays; too many give up after two or three

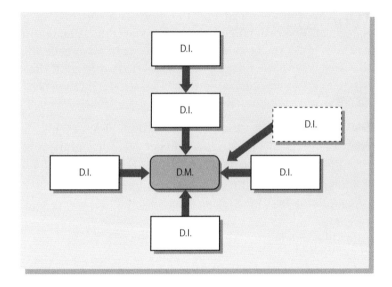

attempts whilst there is evidence that if you keep going for five or more attempts you can win through.

A way of thinking about the typical roles people might have in the overall buying process can be to think of them in these categories:

Initiators: They trigger the need or want. These might be within the customer organisation or in yours if you have people doing marketing or product development. They may be specifiers for a product or service, defining what it has to have or do. It could even be a wider, less specific type of initiator such us 'others are doing it, we have to' – not being left behind. Another possible initiator could be your customer's customers.

Influencers: They have either a direct or indirect influence on the final decision. They may be proactive in their influence, or reactive and only give their ideas or opinions when asked. Quite often, they cannot say yes to choosing a supplier or product but they can say 'no'.

Decision maker: The person (or group) who makes the decision to go ahead.

Buyer: This may be rolled into the decision maker role, or is someone with a clear purchasing role who takes the requirement and aims to get the best deal. Do not get caught up in believing that buyers have the final say. Often they have to present their suggestions to someone else, although not always. It can depend on the power of the initiator or specifier.

End users: Who actually uses the product? For example, a retailer's customers will have an influence on what happens in their decisions. After all, if they do not buy the product, why will anyone stock them?

Combine these various roles and you have the Decision Making Unit. How well do you know yours? How many contacts do you have across the unit?

Doing

A mark of the professional seller is that they recognise the need to spread their contact base within their customers, both wider and deeper. The less competent will settle for one or two contacts and usually at too low a level to really make decisions.

A fundamental principle is to aim as high as possible within the prospect or customer organisation. If the senior people do not feel they need to be involved they can point you to the appropriate person, who will usually see you if you have been referred from someone higher up. You need to have done your preparation to identify who you need to approach and with what message. Why should they want to talk to you or see you? What can your product or service do for them or their organisation?

Beware of having too few contacts! You can be very vulnerable in a customer relationship if this is the case. Should your primary contact leave, their replacement might come from within the organisation or outside. One of the first things the newcomer will want to do is make their mark. How do they do this? Often, they look to make changes and prove that they are worthy of the job, or even better than their predecessor. One way is to bring in new suppliers. You could be at risk because you need to establish a relationship with the new person. Another concern is that they may have a preference for another supplier. They take their proposal to the senior management, recommending the change. What will the response be? If the others have no relationship or connection with you or your organisation, they are not likely to object.

On the other hand, if you have developed some level of relationship with a number of the decision influencers they may take your side and defend you, blocking the change. These relationships do not all have to be maintained by you all of the time or on every call. You might encourage contact from other people and functions within your organisation with their counterparts in the customers or prospects.

Even when you think you have a good range of contacts, you can lose out if you do not pay attention to them and stay close if changes happen. At one stage my previous organisation was getting a large amount of business from a major global company. We knew their key decision makers and the close influencers and worked closely with them over several years. However, complacency started to take over! I was spending more time working outside of the UK and neglected to pay attention to the contacts we knew. Initially, one or two moved out into other parts of their business. We were still close enough because they were replaced by people moving up within the team and we knew them. For another year things carried on as usual. Then, the key Decision Maker moved out and their boss went too. The company changed its strategy and the structure of this department. The new boss came from outside and we could not get in to develop a relationship before the changes started. Within months our successful revenue stream was gone. Not because we had been delivering a poor product. We (I) had neglected to understand the DMU and to manage the relationships within it!

There are some ways you can improve your knowledge and management of the DMU and this is really important if you are selling in a B2B market. One straightforward option is to have an organisation chart, which may be different to their full company

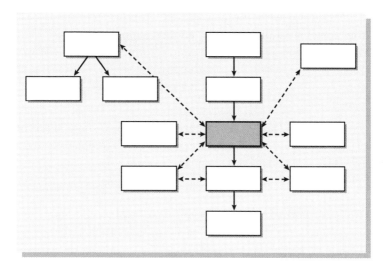

one. You need to know the organisation, and relationships, of those involved in the DMU. There may be some functions or departments which have an influence, even though it is not immediately obvious (e.g. finance have a say if they find you are easy to deal with, accurate with invoicing and resolve queries quickly). Think of these as stakeholders who will be affected by the decision.

In the organogram, you can enter names, even job roles and any other relevant information. A key point is to recognise that gaps are good! Identifying what you do not know means that you can plan to gain the knowledge and fill in the gap. Not acknowledging the gap means that you could be in danger of that person blocking your chances of a sale.

Another option for checking and managing the DMU can be to use a table similar to the one below.

Name	Position	Success factors – decision criteria	Your performance	Their rating	Contacts
Implications and actions					

The two ideas are not mutually exclusive and you can use both with your customer record system. In the table, the success factors column is where you identify what will be important to that person when choosing a supplier or when looking for value. The next one is where you can assess your organisation's performance against these factors. Their rating is to enter how they would rate your organisation (possibly from 0–5). The final column is to encourage you to think about who else from your organisation could be a contact for that customer. When completing this table remember, gaps are good! Those, and what you are able to enter, can prompt some thoughts about what implications you can draw from the exercise and what actions you will take.

The sales person's checklist

- Invest time in understanding the DMU in your prospects and customers. Record the information, either using the ideas in this chapter or in any way which works for you.

- If selling to organisations of any size do not take it for granted that your contact is making decisions on their own. Ask, 'If you want to go ahead, is there anyone else who needs to be involved?' or similar. (Do not ask, 'Can you make the decision?' – you might not always get an honest answer!)

■ Build your knowledge of people's levels of authority in terms of what they can approve or how much they can spend without going up the line.

■ It is probable you will have gaps in your awareness of the DMU. This is good, because you can plan to find out the names and roles and then aim to meet them.

■ Take care if there are new people in the DMU and you do not know them. They may have a relationship with a competitive supplier.

■ Be proactive in monitoring and managing the DMU. It is not a static situation. People move within organisations or come and go, roles and responsibilities change. Ask your contacts about what is happening and to tell you about changes.

■ The balance, or members, of the DMU might change depending on a number of factors, size of order, impact of the decision or length of contract. Keep checking for whether this might happen.

■ When any contact from the DMU leaves, keep a note of where they are going to and get in touch. Who knows, they may be able to use you in their new organisation.

Creating the right first impression

Objectives

- ▣ To appreciate why it is important to manage this step carefully
- ▣ To understand how to present yourself appropriately to create a good impression
- ▣ To recognise how to adapt your initial approach to create the right impression

Understanding

The old saying 'You never get a second chance to make a good first impression' has a lot of truth in it and is very relevant in the sales environment. Whether we like it or not, people make a wide range of judgements when first meeting someone. (You do the same with your prospects!) Even when talking with someone on the telephone the principle is the same, the difference being that our judgements are based only on the voice. There are three key elements to this assessment and initial impression:

1 *You* – do they feel you are someone they can trust and talk to?

2 *Your professionalism* – do they think you will know what you are talking about?

3 *Your organisation* – is it the one they want to deal with?

Varying research suggests that these initial impressions are formed in anything between 7 and 30 seconds. The human eye and mind absorb a great deal of information very quickly and this feeds into our brains where we process and interpret it. We process this data subjectively and irrationally which leads to our conclusions being opinions. There is no point trying to fight this, it is human nature. What tends to happen is that we spend the next period of time with that person reinforcing this first impression. It is not impossible to reverse this impression if you are willing to be patient, persevere and be adaptable in your approach. However, it is preferable to get it right first time more frequently, especially in the sales environment where you do not often get the opportunity to go back and work on building a better impression.

You can influence these first impressions in several ways, starting with your own preparation. Knowing where you are going, what you want to achieve and having the right support material will help to build your confidence. In turn, this will underpin how you come across to others. If someone perceives you as lacking confidence, how confident will they be in considering doing business with you?

When we meet anyone for the first time we build our initial impression from what our eyes see, closely followed by what our ears hear. Most of our information is drawn from the non-verbal signals we receive. We take note of the other person's overall appearance, including their posture and how they are dressed. Body language will play a significant part in the messages and tone of voice rounds them off. Any lack of confidence will be projected through posture, gestures and voice and these signals will be picked up unconsciously by the other person and contribute to the impression they form. If the prospect feels you lack confidence it is unlikely that they will want to open up to you. This will shape their opinion of your capability and professionalism, and through this whether your organisation is one they want to buy from.

Doing

Start by thinking about what sort of impression you want to create. This might sound simplistic, but you may need or want to project different impressions depending on the level of person you are seeing and the type of organisation you are contacting. These principles will apply whether you are making contact by telephone or face to face. Apart from letting the prospect or customer feel you are confident, how else would you want them to perceive you?

When I was on the road selling, my contacts ranged from maintenance engineers working from their offices in a basement several floors below ground level through middle managers to senior managers and directors of medium and large 'City' companies. Although I wanted each to feel I was professional, confident and competent I adapted my approach depending on their role. I was more 'polished' with the more senior levels and more casual and easy-going when talking to the maintenance engineer. In one particular customer, I used to aim to arrive at their tea break and often joined in the card games with the maintenance teams. With the more senior contacts, I definitely adopted a different approach and style of conversation. Looking back on it, this was partly because when starting out in sales, I felt more comfortable with the engineers. However, with time and experience I began to feel equally at home regardless of who I was meeting and I was becoming more confident in myself and what I was doing.

Make sure you have done the appropriate preparation and have the information and support sales material you need. Any doubts about this will undermine your confidence. Now pay attention to you. Regardless of your mood of the day, your journey, or how you slept you need to be able to take a positive professional sales attitude with you when meeting prospects. Tiredness, grumpiness or anything flattening your approach will create the wrong type of first impression and may cause any call or meeting to be cut very short. Managing your own state and mindset is an essential quality for success in sales. This includes paying attention to your 'self-talk' and the messages you are giving yourself. Make sure it is what you want to achieve, think and talk about the outcome you want and avoid thinking about what you do not want. (Avoid the 'don't do this', 'I mustn't ...', because using these sorts of phrase means you have to think about it happening in order to delete the thought and you may find that the initial thought becomes the reality.)

There are two key elements to consider when thinking about you. First, what are you planning on wearing? In the previous chapter I mentioned that you need to dress appropriately. How formal or informal will depend on what market you are selling in and what will fit with the prospects' expectations. These days there is less requirement to be highly formal; not every sector demands suits for each gender of sellers. However, you do need to be presentable and smart. Create a wardrobe of clothes that is appropriate for your sector, feels comfortable to wear and you feel good in because this will influence how you project yourself. You do not have to be overly conservative, nor too flashy or eccentric! The crumpled look will not engender more sympathy and sales. Even if you do not think it matters, it is surprising how many people still check shoes and notice whether they are clean, dirty or scuffed. What impressions will they form? Remember, 'Clothes maketh the man' as Polonius suggested in Shakespeare's *Hamlet*.

Take a few minutes to think through what you want to achieve and how you will do it. Visualise or imagine things going well and having a positive outcome. You want to make sure you are in the right frame of mind to present yourself confidently. Whether you are about to pick up the telephone or walk through a door, be confident, positive and look forward to the call. This will influence how you will be seen by the prospect.

Your tone of voice will be one of the first things to signal your confidence level. If you are nervous your throat tightens, your breathing is shallow and the resulting tone of voice is likely to be scratchy or waver and, possibly, your speech will be a bit rushed. Not the right first impression to give if you want the prospect to believe in your professionalism. Your posture will influence how you sound. Sitting or standing, keep your torso up and allow your chest to expand as you breathe. (This applies whether you are working on the telephone or visiting prospects.)

When going to meet your prospects, approach their premises and them as though you have every right to be there. Avoid acting hesitantly. If talking to a receptionist or security person, be pleasant and firm in asking for information or your contact. As you move on to meeting the prospect, approach them with your head up, and pay attention to the three key things which we all consider when forming our first impressions:

1 *Eye contact* – a level gaze, eye to eye. (Think how you feel if someone does not hold your gaze, but looks away.)

2 *Facial expression, especially a smile* – a pleasant, open look with a slight smile.

3 *Handshake* – we make a variety of judgements based on firmness of grip, dry or damp hands being some of the factors. (Bear in mind that there are cultural differences in expectations and styles of handshake.)

To help generate the impression you want, take the initiative at this first contact.

1 Walk towards the prospect.

2 Establish eye contact, smile and extend your hand as you do this.

3 Check the other person's name, e.g. 'Mr Simon Jones?'

4 Immediately follow on with your own name and the organisation you are from.

5 Thank them for seeing you – and tell them why you are there.

You will find this is easier to do if you know that your preparation has been thorough and you know you have what you need for the meeting.

The sales person's checklist

▓ A key to creating a good first impression is confidence. In turn confidence comes from knowledge. Work at developing your product, customer and market knowledge.

▓ There is no short cut for effective preparation. Identify what elements you need to cover in preparing for calls, plan to do so and then make time for this important activity.

- The more calls you make, the more confident and competent you will become.

- If working mainly on the telephone, make sure you are well set for the calls. Have any material to hand, customer data easy to access on screen if relevant, and your workplace organised.

- Think about how you want to open the calls, how you want to sound. Sit up and have your head up so that you can breathe easily and your vocal cords are not scrunched up.

- For face-to-face selling, make sure your choice of clothes is appropriate for your marketplace and their expectation. If in doubt, be slightly more formal rather than too casual. Having said this, choose clothes which you feel good wearing.

- Get used to walking into prospects' workplaces (or homes) and feeling comfortable and taking the initiative from initial greeting to starting the sales process.

- Enjoy the challenge of creating a good first impression with a wide range of different people and in varied situations. It can be a stimulating part of the job if you adopt this attitude.

Establishing the relationship

Objectives

- To understand the importance of getting into rapport
- To know how to develop your flexibility in order to gain rapport quickly and effectively
- To be able to start to build trust with a wide range of prospects

Understanding

In Part one, we talked about selling being 'to convince of value' and that the person who defines value is the prospect or customer. In order for them to feel they want to share this information we need to establish the right level of relationship and degree of trust. (Remember, they define the levels when these have been reached.) To achieve this, the first challenge is to establish rapport. What is it? It is certainly a word which is frequently heard in the sales context and yet not really understood by most. A full definition is: 'The ability to secure another's attention and to create in them the belief/trust that you have the knowledge, expertise, interest and understanding to assist them. It is the ability to recognise, express and enter into without judgement, the other's model of the world. Rapport is not necessarily about liking or being comfortable.'

My simpler version is 'being on the same wavelength'. Establishing rapport creates an environment of trust and confidence and encourages more openness and participation.

Many successful sales people have the ability to get into rapport quickly with a wide range of different contacts. It is something you have almost certainly been doing in many situations without realising it. Having rapport is what enables us to get along with people. We naturally have rapport with people we like. Where we have little or no rapport communication is a struggle, or even non-existent and there is little chance of trust developing. Think about it as one person tuning into FM radio bandwidth and the other to AM waveband. Each might think they are communicating, because they are transmitting, however the other is not able to receive their signals.

Developing your rapport building skill is fundamental for your sales success. It is essential for establishing the relationship with the prospect and underpins the overall sales process because it is the first step and without it you will not make much progress. Although it is something we all do much of the time in our interactions, there are times when we struggle to achieve it. If this is the case, you will find it virtually impossible to achieve a sale. Liking the other person is not a prerequisite for establishing rapport. What is important is creating effective communication and this is where rapport skills are invaluable.

You can improve your rapport building with practice. Although you have these skills when interacting with most friends and colleagues, you are not conscious of what actually happens when getting into rapport. You will be operating at the 'unconscious competence' stage and achieving rapport automatically. The good news is you can use your skills more effectively to gain rapport with anyone you want to, providing you are open to doing so.

To get into deep rapport with someone else can be very rewarding and intense. In your own personal life this might be enjoyable and a desirable situation. At work, especially in sales, it is not usually necessary to get into this depth. You need enough rapport that the prospect, or prospects, feel you are able to at least really appreciate their position. This can be achieved by a combination of the right skills and attitude from you.

One of the key elements for developing rapport is flexibility in your approach and mindset. It is about adapting to suit the other person and what they require so they start to feel you are focused on them. This will enable them to begin to feel confident in you and begin to trust you. As this builds, so the rapport strengthens and the process becomes circular.

There are a number of things you can do to improve your rapport building and the good news is that you can practise them in all areas of your life rather than solely when you are contacting your prospects. Use your own observation skills to pay attention to people when you are out and about, or watching television. Notice that when people appear to get on well together they often seem to be imitating each other. On the other hand, when people are not getting on well together they stand differently, speak at different volumes and speed and so on. This principle is referred to as mirroring or matching. It is something which happens naturally when we feel we are in rapport with someone. As well as appearing to be matching many aspects of body language when in rapport you will find that you are almost certainly doing the same vocally in volume, speed and even intonation.

Doing

A primary objective for developing rapport is for the prospect to feel as though you are interested in them and their situation. It will help them to become more comfortable about communicating with you and to start to develop trust. When you meet someone it is important to assess them and their style quickly. Recognise the difference between those who want to get down to business quickly and others who prefer to chat more generally first. Adapt your approach to suit them. This is one of the first stages of matching and getting it wrong means you are mismatching – making rapport difficult to achieve.

Avoid doing what I was trained to do, years ago before we understood this. The old cliché about body language held that if the prospect had their arms folded they were being defensive. (Forget the idea of looking for clusters of signals.) To open them up, we needed to 'break' the folded arms and we aimed to achieve this by using a sample of the product and handing it to the prospect in such a way that they would instinctively take it. Some of the time this worked and the prospect would look at specific features, with my help. Looking back, I wonder how many times it only created additional barriers by mismatching the prospect and preventing reaching any real level of rapport? To make it worse, we were intruding into their 'intimate zone' too! Knowing what I know now, there are many better ways of building rapport and gradually moving the prospects by matching them and achieving more successful sales.

When meeting anyone for the first time, pay attention to whether you feel you are getting into rapport. How do you know this is happening? How do you feel? You probably notice that you begin to feel more comfortable and able to communicate more easily. If this is not happening it is an indication that the prospect will not be sensing that they are in rapport with you either.

There are a number of things you can do to build rapport with people. To improve your chances it will help if you are willing to be more flexible in your approach and adapt your behaviour to fit with others. This does not mean you are being weak. Openness and flexibility are strength, not rigidity. Be clear about your initial objective (to build rapport and establish a relationship) and keep your focus on achieving that by doing whatever is required.

Earlier I mentioned the concept of matching or mirroring. Remember, we do this naturally much of the time. However, it is useful to think about it when you are struggling to get into rapport. Pay attention to how you can match:

Element	Specific aspect	Detail
Body language	Posture	How upright, relaxed, sitting or standing?
	Orientation	Face on, angled to each other (imagine there is a line bisecting you and be balanced either side).
	Gestures	Arms and hands - positioning and movement. You do not have to have an exact match, but take care not to mismatch.
		Legs - crossed or not. Similar principle to the arms and hands.

Element	Specific aspect	Detail
	Facial expression	If they look serious avoid smiling and looking cheery and vice versa.
	Eye contact	Establish initial eye contact, then take care to match the prospect. Some find it uncomfortable to hold it. If they look away, do the same from time to time rather than staring.
Vocal (these apply to both telephone and face-to-face situations)	*Breathing*	Believe it or not, when in rapport breathing rates often match. To be fair, this will happen when you have the other parts in sync.
	Volume	Some people speak loudly, others softly. Adapt your volume control to meet theirs.
	Pitch	High, low or in-between. If you are at one end of the register, play around and find ways to modify it slightly.
	Tone	What emotion is being expressed in their intonation? Do they sound angry, upset, bored, enthusiastic? Tune in to identify this so that you can acknowledge their feeling at least.
	Tempo	The speed of speech is one of the key steps towards rapport building. If they are slow and seem to like pauses, match them. Avoid the trap of hoping your enthusiasm will inspire them to speed up! Over time, they might move a bit once rapport is established.
	Words	When the other aspects are working well, it can be very helpful to use people's own words back to them. Also, if you can identify their preferred patterns and use the appropriate language. (Are they more visual, auditory or kinaesthetic?)

When you first meet the prospect, aim to get them talking generally even just for a short time if they seem to want to move straight into business. It is important to let them begin to relax and for you to avoid leaping in with a sales pitch. A useful skill for any seller is to be able to identify appropriate ice breakers. These vary depending on your market, types of prospect and sales approaches. After the general courtesies around your introduction, in a business environment it is often useful to think what areas people will be comfortable talking about. These will tend to cascade from talking about their organisation, followed by their role and experience and lastly themselves. Whilst they are doing this you can build rapport by being genuinely interested and checking how well you might be matching the prospect, making any necessary adjustments. Do pay attention to the overall impression you are getting from the prospect and make this stage as long or short as they want to make it. If you sense things are going well you are probably matching without having to think about it.

For those of you making the contacts by telephone, please think about effective ways of starting your call, preferably avoiding the 'Hello Graham, how are you today?' It rarely sounds as though the caller is really interested and sounds too much part of a poorly written script. Listen closely to how someone answers the phone and aim to match voice tone and speed. Pay attention to any clues which might indicate whether the person is busy, with someone or otherwise engaged and check if it is a good time to talk. You are more likely to start to gain some level of rapport, rather than with some 'cheesy' scripted opening.

The sales person's checklist

- Improve your observation skills to pick up more cues and clues from how people are behaving and the way they are speaking. Practise by taking time to watch people in all environments.

- Think about the people with whom you feel you have a good rapport. What is it that enables you to feel this way? Notice how you are when with these people. Can you spot how you are mirroring or matching each other?

■ When looking at others interacting focus on when and how they mirror and match. Also, notice what is happening when they do not. How well do they appear to be communicating?

■ Look for opportunities to practise your mirroring and matching (of body language and vocal elements.) Experiment with people you know initially, and then with strangers in a non-work environment.

■ Practise, or notice, mismatching and see what happens to any rapport or ease of communication.

■ Work on your flexibility in interacting with others, even if you have to move from your comfort zone. Adapt your voice speed and volume where necessary, change your personal style of movement or gestures to match the other. It might seem awkward to start with, which is natural. It will become easier with time and practice.

Learn more by listening

Objectives

- To understand why listening is critical to effective selling
- To know how to make yourself a better listener
- To use the key elements of active listening to encourage prospects to open up

Understanding

One of the biggest mistakes made about professional sales people is the assumption that they are extroverts who talk a lot. The reality is towards the opposite end of the scale. The majority of consistently successful sales people understand the concept 'We have two ears and one mouth so that we can listen twice as much as we speak' (Epictitus or Socrates). Too many inexperienced or less than successful sellers fall into the trap of talking too much, especially in the early stages of their sales calls. Whether this is due to nerves or a misunderstanding about what they need to do does not matter. Talk too much and you will limit your possibilities for winning business. Remember, salesmanship is about persuading or influencing someone to buy. You need to understand what the prospect thinks is value and they need to feel that they have rapport and the right relationship to share this with you. Knowing you are listening to them will help this.

Listening is very simple, yet hard to do well. Ask yourself, how many people you interact with in your life would you say are really good listeners? If it is more than a handful you are very lucky.

First, you need to recognise that there is a difference between hearing and listening. Hearing is one of the five senses and is a physiological function recognising sounds. Listening is a mental and emotional activity which involves processing verbal and non-verbal messages. In order to listen properly you need to engage with the speaker and give them your full attention. In my opinion listening is an attitude first and foremost. There are skills you can apply to improve your effectiveness as a listener. However, if your attitude is not right and your focus elsewhere than the speaker, these skills will be no help: 'You cannot truly listen to anyone and do anything else at the same time' (M. Scott Peck, *The Road Less Travelled* (1978)).

Second, becoming a good listener can be achieved with a little practice and self-discipline. Even better news, you can practise anywhere and everywhere. This is not something which only applies to the workplace; it is useful in all aspects of your life. A real bonus from being a good listener is that you will find it easier to develop rapport with others and get people to relate to you more easily. If you are lucky enough to know anyone whom you consider to be a good listener, how do you feel when you are going to interact with them? Why is this?

That listening is so important may appear contradictory to how you think about sales and selling. Think back to what we have already covered – selling is convincing of value, influencing people to buy and we need to establish a relationship to build rapport and trust. You will achieve all of these far more easily by listening than by talking about your product or service.

Doing

Developing your ability as a listener starts with deciding that you want to improve. Be aware of your own limitations or bad habits which interfere with your listening. Read through the questions below:

- When you face a problem do you often react before gathering all the facts?
- If someone is speaking do you finish their sentences to speed things up?
- At meetings, once you have made your presentation or statement do you have a tendency to switch off?

- Do you find yourself focusing more on the *way* people say things (grammatically, or words they use) than on the content of their message?
- Do you find yourself interrupting others rather than letting them finish?
- Do you often re-word sentences or find yourself correcting words people use while they are in conversation with you?
- Are you talking more than listening?
- Do you feel the need to fill a pause or gap in conversations?
- Are you often so busy thinking of what you are going to say next that you stop listening to the other person in the meantime? (Waiting for your turn to speak?)
- Does your mind wander when you should be listening, and daydream instead?
- Do you find it difficult to keep looking at the person talking to you?
- Do you find yourself switching off part way through the other person's statements because you think you know what they are going to say?

If you recognise yourself in several of these, you can identify some immediate areas for improvement. As you can see, these all relate to your attitude about the speaker, their message and you. They are not specific skills.

There are some specific behaviours you can use to help you to listen more fully.

- Decide to make the speaker the focus of your attention.
- Resist the temptation to be doing something else at the same time (especially if interacting on the telephone).
- Put aside laptops or other items which might distract you.
- Give eye contact, and hold it to the appropriate degree.
- Be patient – and let the other person finish before you speak.
- Remember, it is the quality of the interaction rather than quantity.

You can also apply the principles and skills of active listening to be even more effective. These do need your attitude to be right for them to work, though. Otherwise, you will not appear genuinely interested and possibly appear insincere. There are three key elements to active listening:

1 *Comprehending* – taking in the message and making sense of it, leading to understanding.

2 *Retaining* – remembering the different parts of the message.

3 *Responding* – giving the speaker some acknowledgement and response, either verbal or non-verbal, to indicate your degree of understanding or checking and questioning if there is an area you want to clarify.

The type of response you make indicates the degree of active listening.

1 *Repeating* – using the person's own words back to them exactly as stated.

2 *Paraphrasing* – using similar words and phrases to show you are thinking about and interpreting their message.

3 *Reflecting* – using your own words to check understanding and to illustrate how closely you were listening.

Some other specific ideas which really strengthen your listening start with you having confidence to clarify what you thought were the main points and ensuring your understanding. Build on the other person's ideas or arguments with your own thoughts ('and' not 'but'). It is not about knocking down their ideas and putting in yours. Show support by encouraging them to continue. You can do this verbally and non-verbally with signals such as nods, sounds of agreement. Finally, help them to develop their ideas with positive questions and using summaries of the main points and actions at regular intervals.

The sales person's checklist

- Make the decision to become a better listener. Start to practise with friends, family and colleagues.

- Use the checklist for listening habits and identify which ones apply to you. Decide on specific actions to address each of these and work on them one by one for a week at a time until you have started to develop a new habit.

- If you know anyone whom you think is a good listener, 'model' them. Notice what they do and how they approach listening. What specific behaviours do they use? If you feel confident enough ask them about how they do it.

- As you improve your listening by giving focused attention, notice how your rapport development gets even better. You will find matching starts to happen more naturally.

- Concentrate on letting people finish speaking before you ask or say anything. You will get more information this way.

- Use both the verbal and non-verbal elements of active listening to encourage the speaker to keep going and to elaborate on what they are saying.

- Remember you listen with your eyes as well as your ears.

three

Making the sale

Questions are your friend

Objectives

- To understand the difference between open and closed questions
- To be able to structure questions in order to build your information from the prospect
- To develop your understanding of the prospect's situation through better questioning
- To create opportunities through effective questioning

Understanding

Many inexperienced, or under-confident, sales people make the mistake of thinking that by talking they are in control of the conversation. This means that they feel the need to keep talking about their product or service, hoping they will strike a chord with the prospect. There is an old saying in the sales world, 'telling is not selling'. Bear in mind you want to influence people to buy something, not feel as though they have been sold it.

Why are questions important?

- You need to develop trust and establish a relationship with the prospect.
- You need to get information from the prospect.
- You need to understand their situation, their priorities and their idea of value.
- You have to be able to tailor your sales message to suit the prospect's requirements.

None of the above can be achieved if you are doing the talking. The only people who have the information you need are not on the sales side of the interaction. Questions will help you to develop trust and build rapport by taking an interest in the other person. As they relax and feel more trusting they will be more willing to share information with you, although this might take more than one call or meeting with some people.

Take care if you are asked, 'Tell me about your …' This might seem like a golden opportunity to enthuse about how great your product or service is. The risk is that you will naturally start emphasising what the organisation does, and especially the aspects you really believe in and think are the strengths. What happens if this does not relate to what the prospect is interested in? There will be times when you have to make an instant judgement about how to respond if you are asked to tell the prospect something about the organisation or your product. Occasionally, you might need to offer some information but take care because you are shooting in the dark. When you are asked something similar to this question, answer in one of two ways. Either, have a short, snappy summary of what you do and what other customers have got from using you. Or, ask the prospect, 'What, specifically, are you looking for from …?' or a variation which you feel comfortable with.

A few years ago I had arrived to run a training workshop on Leadership and Teambuilding for a group of managers from a bank in the Middle East. On the evening before starting, a colleague and I were due to be shown around the resort we were at with some of the senior staff from the bank. Within minutes of being introduced the Head of Retail Banking asked me, 'Tell me, what sort of other training does your organisation provide?' Was it a genuine buying signal and expression of interest? The organisation I was working for probably offered hundreds of training workshops if I had counted them. Where would I start? Bearing in mind I had only met this man minutes before and we had little chance to develop rapport (especially by Middle Eastern standards) it might have seemed politer to offer some sort of information. Instead, I replied with a question. 'I could spend the whole time of our tour listing and explaining the training we can provide. Rather than do that, tell me what specific areas you are interested in, and what prompted your question?' We laughed about the idea of me going through the catalogue and moved on to a more specific answer. To cut the story short, I found out about the new sales strategy and approach they were planning to introduce, what they wanted to achieve and how. This led to a proposal and subsequent work which lasted for several years on and off plus a number of new projects within the bank. Total value was in the mid–high six figures.

Within the topic of communication, there are a number of different types of question which you can use. However, when interacting with other people you are unlikely to be able to remember the labels or think about which specific type of question to use. In sales, the usual questions are 'open' and 'closed'. In principle, 'open' questions will get you information and cannot just be answered with a yes or no. 'Closed' questions can get a yes or no response or a specific answer. Another type of question which some sales people use, and many TV interviewers, is 'leading'. As the name implies, they are aiming to lead the response, e.g. 'Wouldn't you agree that …', or 'I imagine that it is important for you to …'. Although there is nothing intrinsically wrong in these, I feel that they are manipulative and best avoided. Some prospects may feel that you are forcing them into certain answers.

Doing

When looking at questioning, the concept of funnelling is often talked about. There is a logic to this. However, rather than getting too caught up with what questions to ask, put your attention to *how* you ask them. When we communicate in a face-to-face situation only 7% of the impact of our message is delivered through the words. The remainder is made up from the non-verbal mix of voice and body language. (This book is not here to defend the split between words and the rest: even if you want to treble the word impact, it is still a lot smaller than

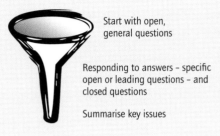

Rapport build to get the prospect to talk openly and comfortably

Start with open, general questions

Responding to answers – specific open or leading questions – and closed questions

Summarise key issues

the non-verbal part.) On the telephone, the words account for 16% and the vocal elements the remainder. Therefore, the way you ask the question, combined with how well you are listening, will have a significant impact on the quality of response you get. Certainly, it makes sense to aim to use open questions, especially in the early stages of the call. To help you remember the starting point for doing this, keep in mind:

> I have six honest serving men
>
> Who taught me all I knew
>
> What, why and when,
>
> How and where and who.
>
> Rudyard Kipling, 'The Elephant's Child',

Examples of open questions could include:

- 'Tell me – what type of work do you do most of the time?'
- 'How do you find the market at the moment?'
- 'When you choose which IT support companies to use, what is important to you?'
- 'Where are you targeting your growth areas?'
- 'Who do you see as your main competitors?'
- 'Why do you think that you have been successful with that product?'

Closed questions will get you a limited response or some level of commitment. There are many ways of starting them. Examples are:

- 'Which would you prefer, A or B?'
- 'Have you any preference for a particular service offer?'
- 'Will you consider us for future requirements?'
- 'Do you use the information we give you with our newsletter?'
- 'Can you see any opportunities for us to supply you?'

It might be preferable to follow the funnel principle and flow from the broad, open questions through to closed ones to tie things down. However, it does not mean that a sales meeting will go perfectly if you do this, especially if you are not listening with total attention. Nor does it mean that things will fail if you do not do so. The important point is to ask questions and more questions. (Remember, two ears and one mouth!)

When doing your pre-call preparation, identify the blocks of information you want to explore or understand and note those down. My recommendation is that you avoid listing questions you want to ask, because there might be a danger that you look on those as a checklist to work through rather than responding to the prospect's answers. Approach the call with curiosity and the questions will flow.

A typical new or nervous sales person might follow this process:

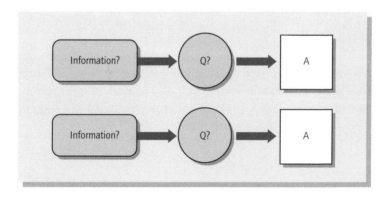

They know what they want to explore, plan the question, ask it and get an answer. They then move on to the next question. In reality, the answer they get is very rarely, if ever, the full picture of the information. This leads to them filling in the gaps for themselves, either basing it on experience from other sales calls or just guesswork.

A better approach to asking questions is shown here, where you want to build and check your information:

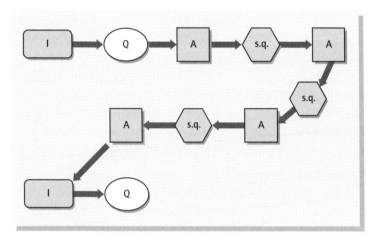

Instead of stopping after the first answer (A), use what the prospect has told you and ask a supplementary question (s.q.) to expand or probe deeper. This is even more effective if you can use some of the prospect's own words when asking the question. It really reinforces that you have been listening closely to what they were saying, which deepens the rapport and encourages them to respond again. As you can see from the diagram, you continue to use supplementary questions, building on the answers until you are confident you have a clear understanding of the information you want. Then you move on to the next block of information. By listening closely you will find that the questions will seem to appear without you needing to worry about whether they are open or closed.

There are various models for structuring your questions. One which I use with organisations looking to use a solution or consultative selling approach is:

P – ask about what is happening at **Present**.

I – what **Issues** are they facing?

C – what are the **Consequences** of these issues?

K – check your **Knowledge** and understanding of these.

S – begin to identify your **Solutions** in concept and discuss with the prospect.

The sales person's checklist

- Take any opportunity to practise your questioning skills, with friends, family or colleagues. Remember to link this with your listening practise as the two go together.

- Any time someone is talking to you or explaining things, focus on asking questions for clarification or to get a fuller understanding. Resist the temptation to fill in any gaps for yourself by guesswork.

- Use the 'building information' process whenever you get the chance so that you develop this as a natural way of interacting with others.

- Watch colleagues or others, such as TV interviewers, when they are asking questions and notice whether they are using closed or leading questions. Also, how often do they interrupt the other person? What happens to the flow of the conversation?

- When preparing sales calls identify two or three specific areas of information you want to explore. Trust yourself to find the right questions.

- Work to avoid the three mistakes – doubling up questions (asking a second one before the prospect has had a chance to answer the first one); interrupting them; and using leading questions.

It's not what it is, it's what it does

Objectives

- To understand the concept of benefit selling
- To understand the difference between features, advantages and benefits
- To be able to match benefits to needs

Understanding

In Part one the first item listed under the knowledge required was 'product – application'. This term was included deliberately. Too often sales people, and others in their organisations, think that they need to know all about the products or services. The drawback with this is that prospects are not interested in what your product or service is. They want to know what it does, or can do, for them. How will it help them to meet their needs and wants? You need to imagine each person you are selling to is asking, 'What's in it for me?' Think about what you consider when buying something. If you are looking for a smart phone, what matters to you? Screen size, number of pixels for the camera, size of keypad, access to e-mail, having FM radio, or …? The inexperienced seller will tell you enthusiastically about these and many other things which the phone possesses. Are you interested in all of them or only a few or any? You want to know about the parts which will be relevant to you and how you want to use the device. The other, irrelevant points are not seen as added value.

Too much marketing and promotional information gives lists of the features of the product or service, hoping that the prospect will make the leap to understanding how these will help them or their company. Unfortunately, most of the time people do not make the connection. They want to know how it will relate to them and their idea of value. Even when information tries to talk about benefits it is not really offering those.

The term 'benefit selling' is often heard in the sales environment, for good reason. People make their buying decisions when they perceive that the benefits of the product or service meet their value criteria. What are benefits? To establish these we need to go back a step or two and understand some sales terminology.

Features: These are facts about your organisation, products or services. They are not opinions or beliefs.

Advantages: These are derived from the feature and are available to the market as a whole.

Benefits: Advantages which match an expressed or explicit need.

Too many sales people work hard at developing their product knowledge and this leads to them learning a list of features. At one level this is a good thing. However, there are two risks with this idea. There is a natural temptation to focus on the features which you believe are the best or feel most comfortable with. The other problem is there can be a tendency to deliver this list with enthusiasm without checking whether it resonates with the prospect. The trouble is that sometimes it does work, so the seller thinks it is the way to talk about their offering. Despite these risks, you do still need to know the features thoroughly.

When learning your features it is also useful if you can identify any USPs (Unique Selling Points) you may have. These can be extremely useful if you have any for your organisation, products or services because they are a source of differentiation and can give you an edge over competition. However, being realistic, USPs are not easy to find or sustain as many people claim. Even if you have some, they may not be useful if they cannot be translated into benefits, meeting a prospect's needs.

I recall in my earlier selling days falling into the traps outlined here. We were trained to learn the features of our products and the USPs were emphasised. I think there were four or five which I really thought were great and worth stressing. Call after call I would draw the prospect's attention to these features and what I thought were the benefits. In truth, they were advantages not benefits. Yes, they worked some of the time, but I wonder how much more successful I would have been if I understood the real process of benefit selling and established the needs more clearly?

Doing

Once you have learned your feature library you need to know how to use the features to sell the benefits. There is a simple process to follow, the FAB formula (Feature → Advantage → Benefit).

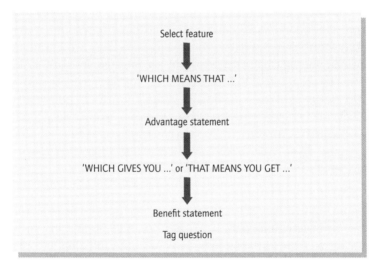

Select feature

↓

'WHICH MEANS THAT ...'

↓

Advantage statement

↓

'WHICH GIVES YOU ...' or 'THAT MEANS YOU GET ...'

↓

Benefit statement

Tag question

Thinking about the smart phone scenario, let us try this out.

Feature It has a large 4.8-inch screen *WHICH MEANS THAT ...*

Advantages   ... it is easy to read e-mails or messages

... it is easy to view photographs you have taken or received

... you can watch film or TV clips or programmes easily

... when browsing the internet you can see the pages

(You might be able to identify some more advantages. I believe that most features will have three to six advantages. Remember, these are of limited use if they cannot be moved through to becoming benefits.)

WHICH GIVES YOU ...

Benefit   ... the ability to research your prospects when on the move

... the opportunity to access your CRM system and see the customer information

(These will only be benefit statements if the prospect stated they wanted to be able to check prospect information, or to access the CRM system when on the move.)

Tag question – 'Is that the sort of thing you are looking for?' or 'Does that give you the CRM access you want?'

The tag question is meant to be a closed one. If you do not get a positive response, the prospect has not bought the benefit. Even a hesitant response is not ideal, although not bad news. This means you need to find another feature – advantage – benefit to fully meet the need.

In an earlier chapter I had recommended that you write down the prospect's 'shopping list' and make sure you qualify each point too. One of the reasons was to give you thinking time. As you are noting down each item, you need to think backwards. You know what benefits the prospect is seeking. From here you can go to what advantages will provide these benefits. Once you have worked this out, identify which features have these advantages. In your early stages of a sales career you might find it helpful to note which features you want to use. You are now ready to go with your 'FAB formula'.

I have been saying throughout that the aim is to convince of value. Once you know the prospect's shopping list, choose the right features and turn them into the benefits which deliver the needs and wants on the list. This shows how you can deliver value according to their criteria. They will want to buy from you, which is the aim of good salesmanship.

The sales person's checklist

- Invest time in thoroughly learning your feature library, for your organisation, products and services. If it helps, write them down and practise sharing them with someone so that you become confident in your knowledge.

- Identify if you have any USPs and learn those.

- Practise working through the 'FAB formula' process until you are fluent. Get used to the 'which means that ...' and 'that gives you ...' phrases so that they become second nature.

- What are the most frequent expressed needs and wants your prospects state? Thinking of these, and what benefits they are seeking, which features and advantages will deliver them? Familiarise yourself with these so that you can use them confidently.

- Find someone (colleague or friend) who can role play different types of prospects and practise responding to their shopping lists with the FAB formula.

Present your sales case

Objectives

- To recognise when to present your sales case in the sales process
- To identify the pitfalls to avoid
- To develop a specific structure to help you through presenting your sales case
- To make sure you address the requirements of the different people in the DMU

Understanding

There are three key questions to ask about presenting your sales case. When to do it? What to include? How to do it? Too many sales people want to launch into talking about their product or service and think that they can convince the prospect through the power of their argument combined with their enthusiasm. It may work – occasionally. This is where a structured sales process can help, because it positions the presentation in the most effective position.

The way I have suggested you approach sales follows this simple process:

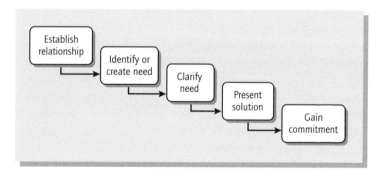

There is no point in presenting your product, service or solutions until you are clear about the needs and wants of the people within the DMU and their value criteria. If you do it before this there is a significant risk that you will miss some key elements for the prospect. You will be trying to sell to them rather than influencing them to buy. Resist the temptation to deliver your sales presentation too early, especially if you have been asked to tell them about what you can offer. There is a difference between giving a succinct overview of what you do and a focused sales presentation.

The good news with using this process is that it also gives you some clues about what to include. Having established and clarified the needs and wants, you have the content for your presentation. If it relates to these and explains how these will be satisfied you are on the right lines. Anything not in those areas of interest is likely to be irrelevant and does not necessarily add to the strength of your sales case.

When ready to present your sales case it will help you to have some structure which can guide the prospects through, showing your understanding of their situation and easing to your solution. You can then provide the proof and rationale with the reasons why they need to go ahead, explaining how you will deliver the value they are seeking.

Doing

The third question was about how to present your sales case. When you have your understanding of the detail you can think about what you need to include and how you will put it across. One way of structuring your presentation is to follow the DIPADA model. This has been around for many years, and comes in and out of favour like many things. The strength of this approach is that it can be used if you are working in telephone sales or face to face, and is applicable on initial calls or follow-up meetings. It is also a good framework for formal presentations and can even help you organise a proposal.

I find it useful to use the actual words of the first three steps to remind me where I am in the presentation and to prevent me rushing on too quickly. The steps are:

D – Define: the situation (or redefine if on a return visit to present a proposal.) Use the prospect's own words and any of their industry terminology. Questioning is the key skill to help you get the information in order to be sure of your understanding. I start by saying something along the lines of, 'Can I just *define* your situation based on my understanding? ...' If going back, I redefine the situation.

I – Identify: the solution in concept. (Only as an idea – not at all product oriented or specific.) 'Let me *identify* the solution I think is right for your situation. I suggest we can do something on the lines of ...' (or) 'What we can do is ... Does that sound like the type of solution you are looking for?' The last question is important. If they do not agree with the solution in concept there is little point in continuing. You need to take this as feedback that you either do not have a full understanding of their situation and what they want to achieve or you have misjudged something. If this does happen, go back and check. There can be a good reason, especially if you are returning for a follow-up call. Things do happen and priorities change.

P – Prove: the solution. 'I would like to *prove* how we will do this.' You then go back to the points you identified on their shopping list and use the FAB formula. (Depending on your product or service, use demonstrations, technical data, cost justification or whatever is appropriate.)

A – Acceptance: gain agreement with each point of proof. You need to see that the proof is being bought into. Observe the non-verbal responses, pay attention to any questions or comments. Check understanding and attitudes with questions and trial closes.

D – Desire: Hopefully, this is being built up as the points of proof are being accepted. You can tell this is happening when you start to pick up buying signals. Use trial closes to check just how warm the prospect is getting.

A – Action: Rather than keep your presentation going on and circling round, when you reach the end of the prove step, ask for commitment or tell the prospects what you need to occur next.

When using DIPADA to address a group, or different people in the DMU, remember to talk about each of their issues or situation in the define step. Similarly, when identifying the solutions acknowledge the potential impact on each of them. Your preparation has to cover this. If you suspect you may have to present to more than one person, check who else will be present. This will also remind you to make sure you have enough copies of any material, literature or samples for each person.

Use the information from your plan to prepare your presentation and the message you want to put across. As you are working through the proof statements make sure that each benefit is related to the specific value criteria for the individuals and use their language or words wherever you can (referring to the notes you may have written).

As you cover the proof statements, be confident and capable when talking about the money side. Be comfortable to talk about costs, returns, margins etc. If you are not, why should they feel confident about your proposal? Be ready to justify your pricing by linking it to their savings or returns, etc.

Make sure your sales case is tailored to suit the prospect and not a standard organisational pitch. The aim of your presentation is to show the prospect you understand their requirements, get an agreement to your solution and then prove how you can deliver it and meet their value criteria. Leading through these steps you have a much better chance of influencing them to buy.

The sales person's checklist

- Make sure you have the prospects' needs and wants identified and clarified before you give any sort of presentation.

- Keep in mind the three key questions: when do I do it, what must it include, and how will I do it?

- When using the DIPADA model, put the headings onto paper to use as a prompt. If you want to add some other information, use bullet points rather than a lot of detail.

- Practise using the model with some colleagues or friends so that you become comfortable with the flow. Check if you find it helpful to use the words as a prompt for the early steps.

- Presenting your sales case may be just a one-to-one conversation or a formal session to a group. It does not matter – the principles are the same.

- Gather any information you can about the financial aspects of your product or service, and the costs for your prospects, when using your product or what you can save them. Fundamentally, know the financial implications thoroughly so that you can give a sound cost justification.

- Learn from each presentation of your sales case by reviewing how it went. Look at those which could have gone better and also at those which were successful. What lessons can you take from each?

- Whether doing a proposal or a presentation, remember to address the 'shopping list' of each person in the DMU.

Handling barriers to the sale

Objectives

- To recognise the message behind the barrier or objection
- To know how to handle barriers in a controlled and confident manner
- To use a structured process for dealing with barriers or objections
- To feel more confident when you encounter objections

Understanding

It is unlikely that you will reach the end of a sales meeting without the prospect or customer raising some barriers, or objections. These will prevent them going forward and actually buying from you. This does not necessarily mean you have done anything wrong. Even if you go through the steps of the sales process effectively, these barriers can still occur. Some might start at the outset with someone not wanting to see you or give you the time you feel you need. There is no one specific time or situation for them to occur within the sales process. Added to this, different personalities will respond in their own way. Some will seem to challenge or question more than others. As your experience develops you will be able to assess individuals more effectively and identify if this is the situation. If you do find you seem to be meeting a lot of barriers or objections it is time to step back and review how you have been approaching the sales call. You may be contributing to the situation.

A few years ago I was asked to go to a meeting with a client who was one of the major banks. They were having a major thrust on selling financial products and services. On arriving, I was told that they wanted me to develop a training programme for their sales people on 'objection handling and closing'. Apparently, someone who I knew from their training team had researched what was happening and reached the conclusion that this was the requirement. The branches were making appointments for customers to see the sales people, who had the meetings but were not converting many to sales.

We had developed, and delivered, some other sales training programmes for the client, which was why they asked me in. I asked why they felt that the issue was around objection handling and closing. They responded by talking about poor conversion rates from meetings to purchases. It took me some time to move their thinking from this, which was the symptom of the problem, not the cause. Eventually, they recognised that the issue started with poorly qualified prospects. (In fact, many were not prospects. They had been talked into the appointment and there were a lot of 'no shows'.) The next step was also overlooked. The sellers were too quick to push products and did not spend time identifying or creating needs. I managed to convince them that the problem was not objection handling and that the solution was to have a workshop which put the emphasis at the front end of the sale not the end. If the early stages are not being handled properly there is little point in learning lots of ways of handling barriers and closing.

When you hear the prospect raise a barrier it is important to avoid becoming defensive. It is not about you, so do not take it personally. Nor are they a challenge to battle through. (The saying 'You may win the argument – and lose the sale' has a lot going for it!)

Objections are raised by prospects for a variety of reasons:

- they want to get rid of you or feel they do not have time to see you,
- they are not convinced by what you have been saying,

- they need more information,
- they feel under pressure to make a decision,
- they haven't yet made up their mind (and may genuinely need more time),
- they have misunderstood something,
- a red herring to deter you,
- a genuine reason for not going ahead.

If a prospect does make any statement which appears to be an objection, take time to think about, what is the message behind it? Which of these does it come from? This can help you in the way you respond and handle it.

Doing

Golden rule 1 – never contradict the prospect directly, even if you can prove that they are wrong in their objection. The title of this chapter is deliberately chosen as handling barriers rather than talking about overcoming objections.

Golden rule 2 – there is no perfect approach for responding to objections and handling them. Even if you think you understand the reason behind it and have used a rational way of dealing with it, you may not be able to convince the prospect.

The first thing to do to prevent objections taking you by surprise is to think about what potential objections might crop up as part of your pre-call preparation. You will find that you can anticipate a significant percentage of objections after a while as you get to know your target customer base. This means you can think about how you will handle the objections if they are raised.

Another benefit of thinking about possible objections before the call is that you can actually pre-empt them by raising them yourself. This might surprise you. It is better for you to bring it up rather than waiting for the prospect or customer to do so. By admitting to the situation you can diffuse a lot of the power of the objection. Simply be open: 'I know we had a situation with ... in the past' or 'I realise you have been using ABC company for some time, and they are a good supplier'. Acknowledging the probable concern can lead to a positive conversation.

Even if you have anticipated the possible objections and some are raised, or if you meet some you have not expected, it is helpful to follow a simple process such as ACER.

A – Acknowledge: Maintain rapport, show understanding of their concern or the barrier. This also demonstrates that you are listening and paying attention.

C – Clarify: Check that you understand what it is they are saying and if you can find the message behind it. You may ask them to repeat the 'barrier', or use a phrase such as 'I would just like to check what you are saying …', 'My understanding is …' or similar.

E – Explore: Question to establish the reasons behind their statement or question: what is it based on, what do they want or expect? It is possible to encourage the prospect to consider options at this stage

R – Respond: When you understand the message behind their barrier and the specific reasons you can respond with a statement, or statements, to convince them why this need not be an issue or how you can deliver what they want. It might be an opportunity for more benefit statements, especially if they have expressed some additional needs and wants during the clarify or explore stages.

A particular objection which you will encounter is around price. Before looking at pointers for dealing with this objection there are a couple of things for you to consider. Be proud of your price! If you do not believe that what you are offering is fairly priced or decent value you will not be able to convince anyone else. Remember, you do not have to be the cheapest to be good value. (If you are always cutting price to be the cheapest, why does your organisation need you to sell? If you are buying business, the organisation needs lower overheads and that means sales people are not needed.) Do not be surprised when a prospect queries your price or raises barriers about it. The question, 'Can you do anything about your price?' is just that – a question. Too many sales people hear this and become defensive or concerned. Many prospects ask this because they know that if they do they may find that the seller will start discounting straight away. Look them in the eye and say a pleasant 'no'. Alternatively, suggest if they buy more or give some decent incentive you may be able to offer something. (Or, my response if I feel the rapport is at the right level, is to look at them, smile pleasantly and say, 'Yes, of course …' and, as they look hopeful, 'how much would you like me to add?' It is not part of everyone's style and it is not meant to be too flippant. It usually raises a laugh, or at least a chuckle, and then we can move on.)

A key point to understand is that there is a difference between price and cost. The price of a product or service is what the buyer pays. The cost is the total expense of using that product over a given period. When facing price objections it is helpful to understand the difference between the two and the principle of cost/benefit analysis. This enables customers to compare the cost with the savings and other benefits they receive, so that they can decide whether the investment is sound. Also, as part of ACER, clarify whether the objection is about your price or the cost. You can build a cost/benefit analysis into your presentation where appropriate and this pre-empts the problem later.

When a price objection is raised it could mean any of the following:

- The prospect is an experienced or professional buyer aiming for a discount.
- The prospect has no budget at the moment (although this should have been checked).
- A competitor has quoted less.
- The product is dearer than expected.
- The customer doesn't like the product or is not convinced of the need.

If it is a genuine price objection, which is usually based on a comparison with an alternative, you can use a four-step method of price justification.

1 **Establish the difference**: Ask what your price is being compared with and calculate the exact difference. (Make sure it is the same specification of product or service.) Remember, you need to justify the difference not your actual price, e.g. £19 v £20 = £1 to justify.

2 **Express the difference in smaller units:** This stage breaks down the difference into smaller amounts or components. For example, it can be divided by the number of years of ownership, or a cost per use or user, cost per day/week/month or occasions when the product will be used, or the number of people it benefits.

3 **Restate the benefits:** Emphasise any benefits that can be expressed in terms of cost saving, still focusing on the difference not your total price. These will enable you to make a direct comparison. Then restate the benefits that are more subjective.

4 **Show that the benefits outweigh the difference:** This is a logical process and should make your sales case. It leads naturally into the close.

The sales person's checklist

- Identify the most frequent objections which occur in your sales environment. Write them down using the specific words which the prospects say. If you work with others, ask for them to add to the list.

- Read each through and identify the reason behind each. How can you identify the actual reason?

- Look at the objections you have listed and imagine working through ACER with each. It is even more powerful if you have somebody to practise with and can role play them. You will improve the more you practise because you will become more fluent and confident.

- Get information about your product usage, lifespan and any other data which you can use as part of your price justification approach. Practise calculations for various sales situations and against different competitors. Initially, do this by writing the figures down.

■ When doing a price justification with a prospect ask for their input on the data for their costs, usage and any other relevant area. They will believe their figures before yours. If they are not certain, know your market well enough to suggest ball park figures.

■ Develop the habit of writing down figures and any calculations related to the justification and doing this so that the prospect can see what you are doing. (Or enter the data on your laptop or tablet if you are using one.)

■ Remember, barriers and objections are not personal.

■ Do not contradict the prospect – you might win the argument, but you will probably lose the sale.

Getting commitment

Objectives

- To recognise when the prospect is indicating interest through giving 'buying signals'
- To know how to build commitment through trial closes
- To confidently ask for the final commitment

Understanding

A number of sales people are reluctant to ask for the order, or close the sale. There are several possible reasons for this:

- They do not want to be rejected.
- They do not want to seem to be pushy.
- They do not feel confident in doing so.
- They do not know how to do it.

These are all understandable. No one likes to be told 'no', nor do they want the prospect feeling that they are being pressurised. Either of these concerns contributes to a lack of confidence and not knowing how to ask for an order would be another factor.

In reality, there is no need to feel any of these concerns if the sales process has been followed. The step of asking for the order should be natural on reaching the conclusion of the process. If you are clear about the prospect's idea of value and have presented your sales case to show how you can give them this they ought to be ready to buy from you. If you have any doubts about asking for the final commitment it could be because you are not sure that the prospect is at this point yet. However, they have probably given you a number of clues during the call.

The graph below shows what happens during the sales call. The wavy line shows what happens to a prospect's interest

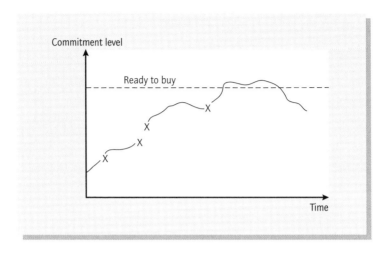

level throughout. You can see that the progress to the 'ready to buy' level does not go smoothly. There can be times it even goes backwards, usually when the prospect is thinking of an objection or has a doubt about something. As their interest level rises they will offer you some indicators that this is happening. These are shown with an X on the graph and are called 'buying signals'. They do not infer that the prospect is ready to buy, more that they have reached another step on the commitment path.

There are a number of ways in which these might occur:

Verbal

- Interest questions – what ones might your prospects ask?
- Some objections – raising barriers to going ahead.
- Intonation – sounding more positive, making 'hmm' sounds.
- Assumed ownership – talking about 'when we start to use …', rather than 'if we start to use …'

Non-verbal

- Moving forward – or backward, some other change in body posture.
- Putting glasses on – or removing them.

- Head movement, e.g. nodding or moving it.
- Reaching for something you have shown, looking through a document or some material, scrolling through the screen.

The prospect will be giving these clues naturally during the call. The challenge for you is to be attentive enough to spot them. If you are too focused on yourself and your sales pitch there is a risk that you will miss them. Your antennae need to be attuned to the prospect. The danger if you do not spot the signals and respond appropriately is that the prospect moves up to the ready to buy level, but if they are not committed their interest wanes and drops away as shown in the graph. This usually happens because the seller is talking too much and is sometimes referred to as 'talking your way into and out of an order'.

It is vital that you become skilled at spotting the buying signals the prospect offers and recognise how their interest level is rising. The next essential step is to know what to do each time you pick up on the clue. You need to establish the commitment level by using a 'trial close'. This is a way of testing where the prospect is and how they are responding to what you are saying. As the interest level builds you move from the trial closes to a final close. The only difference between these is when you are asking them in the call and what you expect the outcome to be.

Doing

A key to asking for commitment at any stage in the call is to feel confident doing so. If you are doubtful this will be projected to the prospect and it is unlikely that they will feel confident in going. By the time they are giving you buying signals you should have a good level of rapport, there is no reason to be uncertain. Think about it, what is the worst which can happen? They say no, or indicate they are not at that level of commitment. This is simple feedback for you. Go back a stage or two until you can re-establish common ground and understanding.

When you spot a buying signal, or think you have, make sure to check it with a trial close. This will be a question to check how the prospect feels or whether they want more information or need something else. Trial closes indicate how the prospect is responding to what is happening and, if used properly, you may find that you can reach the final commitment much earlier than you might have thought.

When you think that the prospect is close to the 'ready to buy' level you need to act. If you are using the collaborative approach which is being encouraged in this book you do not need 15–20 ways of closing the sale. The days of the hard sell and tough close are gone in most sensible sales environments. This does not mean you do not need to ask for commitment when necessary. Some of the time, if you are listening closely, you might find your prospect asking what they need to do or about the next steps if they go ahead. They do the committing for you. However, most of the time you will need to be proactive with this step and it helps to have a few options to use.

Some ways of asking for commitment are shown here and they can be adapted for either trial or final closes.

Direct

Ask for their commitment with a straightforward question. 'Are you interested in going ahead?', 'When would you like to start?', 'Are you happy we have covered everything?', 'I think we have dealt with all of your questions. Shall we get things underway?', 'Is that the sort of service you are looking for?', 'If we can provide that, would you be happy?'

Alternative

Giving a choice, where either response is a positive. 'Would you prefer to have the order sent to one central point or for us to deliver to each plant?', 'Do you want to have just product XXX on this order, or would you like to add the other items too?', 'Would you like them all in the same colour or a mixture?', 'Do you want five or ten?'

Assumptive

A question or statement which assumes that they have agreed and refers to a detail which must be cleared up. (This is the only time you can assume in selling!) 'When we are delivering, will your store be open all day?', 'When the account is set up, will you be the person ordering?', 'How often do you think you will be ordering each month?'

Summary

As the name implies, you summarise all that you have covered and then finish with a direct statement or question. Used well, it involves covering all of the need statements coupled with the FAB points and can be very compelling and powerful. 'Let me just recap, you said you were looking for, and we have ... that gives you; and you wanted, we can do ... giving you ... So we seem to be able to offer all that you wanted, is there anything to stop you going ahead?' (Or 'we have covered everything, shall we get things underway?')

The sales person's checklist

▪ Start looking for buying signals, both verbal and non-verbal. Notice when they occur during the call. What specific clues do the prospects give? As you start this exercise be kind to yourself if you forget to trial close when you spot the signal.

▪ When you can start to spot the buying signals, practise trial closing each one. Keep your focus on the prospect and their responses – they may be closer to committing than you think.

▪ Look at the ideas for ways of asking for commitment and identify the ones you feel most comfortable with. Starting with those, write out some examples in your own words and practise them using friends or colleagues to role play the prospects.

■ After you have one or two closes you are comfortable with, add another, and another. Repeat the previous activity.

■ Review each call and think about what buying signals the prospect gave you. Assess whether you trial closed them and, if you had a chance to reach the buying level, did you ask for commitment. Develop this habit. Where can you improve?

■ Whenever you ask for commitment during the call, be confident and comfortable in doing so. You have every right and reason to ask.

part

four

Setting the sales strategy

The fit between the business strategy, marketing and sales

Objectives

- To understand where the sales function should fit within the overall strategy
- To understand the role of effective marketing analysis and planning in sales

Understanding

Although sales is the most critical function of a business because it brings in the revenue to sustain the operation, it does not operate in isolation and nor should it. Too many times businesses set sales plans (mainly revenue targets) without looking at the bigger picture. This mistake is not just made by small or inexperienced organisations; larger ones fall into the trap too. The target is set using internal criteria for what the management want to achieve. Frequently, they take the last year's results and use those as the basis for the next year and set numbers assuming a mystical growth figure. Some organisations consider a bottom-up approach by asking for input from those doing the selling about their forecasts for the next year. This is commendable in principle. Unfortunately, in practice, this often does not work. If the figures given by the sales people do not equate to the desired target for the organisation they are overlooked and the internal numbers are imposed. A major issue with this is that the sales people are not likely to believe in these targets. This will have implications for their commitment to the figures and their motivation and likelihood of achieving them.

Logically, there should be a clear business strategy providing a sense of direction and overall objectives to be achieved. This ought to be established and written in a business plan which then sets out the financial targets and budget. Too often the budget seems to be the driving force. It focuses on setting a target revenue figure and then looks at the various costs required to run the business. When these figures are finalised, some plans may be produced about how to achieve them. These will be far more tactical than strategic. They are then used as the driver for the sales operation, which may support or sabotage the efforts of the sales people.

A well-constructed business plan can be a powerful foundation for any sales operation. The process shown in the diagram below can be used for establishing the business plan and for the marketing and sales plans.

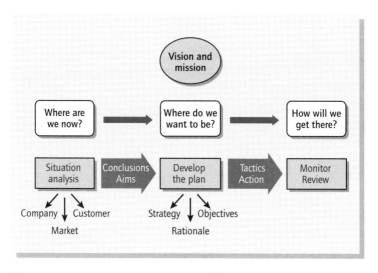

An error too many organisations make is not investing enough time in the overall planning process and especially not at the 'Where are we now?' step. They are too quick to jump to the 'Where do we want to be?' step without really knowing whether they are in a good position to move towards it.

If the organisation does follow this process the business will know where it is and why it is there. There is some debate that the initial work for a marketing plan can be done first to help to provide this foundation. A key element of a professional marketing function is that it invests as much time and energy in analysis and research as, or even more than, the promotion and communication stage. This assessment looks at the strengths and weaknesses of the organisation and other factors which can feed into the business, marketing and sales plans. There should be a natural flow and fit between each of them from the overall broad direction, through the more detailed marketing plan and finally into the sales plan and operational requirements. Where this does not happen a 'disconnect' occurs between the sales plan and activity and the intentions for the remainder of the business. In turn, this can lead to friction between different functions and managers.

Doing

First principle – invest time in the initial stage, situation analysis. Whether as a business, marketing or sales function, this is the critical step. There are three strands:

1   Where are you as an organisation? How is business? Where are you being successful? Where are you struggling? Where can you improve?

2   Who are your main customers? What has been happening with them and their levels of business? How can they be split? (Or, in marketing terms, how are they segmented?) Are there specific types or size of customer where you do better? Is there any geographical pattern?

3   What is happening in your market? What about your customers' marketplace? What are the trends? What have your competitors been doing? How have they been performing?

Although you need to do this with a sales focus, it will be more effective if you ensure your analysis is linked with any which has been done by the business or marketing functions. When you have the basis of a sound situational analysis you can begin to consider the next step of where you want to be. There is no harm in being positive and optimistic in this, but it does help if there is a degree of realism in the aspiration. Knowing this, you can start to develop your plan ensuring that your sales strategy is aligned with the other key plans.

Where does the sales strategy come from?

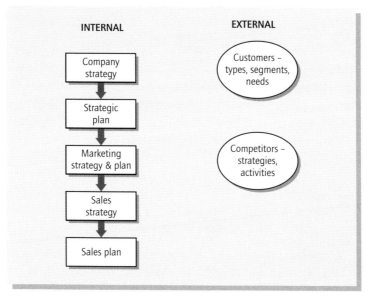

The plan should be a series of natural steps which provide the overall direction and strategy, the specific objectives and the actions required to deliver the results. By making sure it is created within the process shown, your sales plan has a better chance of success. Not only should the way forward be clear and in line with the business aims, the structure and systems should be in place to support and reinforce the sales plan and the sales activities.

The sales manager's checklist

- Before starting on the sales plan check the business plan and marketing plan (if they exist). If neither has been done, at the very least have a conversation about the intended strategy for the organisation and any rationale or analysis behind it.

■ Work with the other functions to share information about the elements involved in the situational analysis.

■ Make sure that you are clear about the target market segments you want to address and focus your activity on those.

■ Set up regular meetings with the other functions to revisit and review the different plans, to discuss progress and to check that they are in alignment.

■ Feed into the other functions what you need from them in order to achieve the sales plan.

Setting the strategic direction

Objectives

- To set the sales direction and routes to market
- To identify the most appropriate sales strategy for your organisation
- To be aware of the implications for involving other areas of the organisation in selling

Understanding

A clear sense of direction will give you a better probability of success with your sales operation. Sales success cannot be achieved in isolation. Although many of the sales activities might be happening physically outside, the internal systems and processes need to be supportive of these efforts. In my experience, this does not happen often enough. Frequently, functions work towards their own aims and objectives without considering any of the others, not just sales. To achieve the sales objectives these elements need to fit together.

The key element in deciding on your sales direction is to be clear about who your target customers are, and the most effective way to reach them. Analysis of the market and competition will help you think about what direction you want to take to reach your target segments. The sales plan should indicate the way you intend to go to the market to achieve the desired results within your budget.

If you are using a 'traditional' field sales approach you need to decide on the specific requirements of the role. These can range from the amount of prospecting, through the actual level of sales activity to designing or developing solutions and the degree of customer service or sales support they are responsible for. How will the sales territory be defined? Is it geographical, or by customer type or some other criteria? How many accounts can someone realistically handle? What size? Do you expect all sales people to handle all types of customer?

Are you thinking of selling indirectly, using distributors, agents or other resellers? What will be your criteria for choosing those for your product or service? Why will they promote you over any other items in their range? What can you provide or offer to encourage them? Although this might seem like an attractive option with relatively low costs and apparently minimal risk, it does have some potential limitations arising from your lack of direct control. Before choosing this route to market, do your homework and research the potential hazards.

Telesales is another option if your product or service can be sold this way. The issue is whether you need out-bound or in-bound calls to generate the sales. The challenges for telesales are different to field sales, although a number of the skills might be similar. For out-bound teams, you need to provide them with a constant stream of suspects to be calling. You also need to implement a good CRM system.

A number of sales organisations combine telesales with field sales operations, whether for appointment making, handling small customers or as part of a sales support function. There can be significant benefits in working this way if you get the structure right.

The sales strategy should influence the direction you set. There are a number of labels which are often heard in this area:

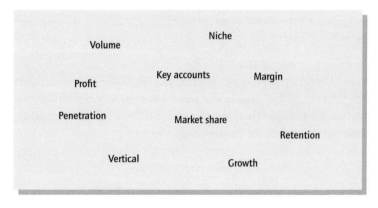

When you have an idea of your sales strategy and direction you can decide how to share this with others in the organisation to make sure they know where they can support the process and possibly contribute positively.

Doing

It is always worth reviewing your sales direction and strategy at least a couple of times a year rather than waiting for the budget time and when you redo your sales plan. In the 21st century most markets are dynamic and both customers and competitors can change what they want or how they operate. Waiting too long to review what is happening can mean you are heading in the wrong direction or get left behind.

Your strategy and direction are interconnected. One will influence the other and also have an impact on it. The outlines below can be used as a defined strategy or they can be combined in many instances.

Volume

If your strategy is about achieving volume of sales it means you need to be proactive in your sales activity to generate opportunities. Whether using field sales or telesales you need to have enough people to pursue this option. You also need to consider having some flexibility in your pricing.

Niche

Focusing on a narrow market where you can position yourselves as experts. This strategy has its advantages because you can usually identify your target customer easily and develop ways to reach them. If your product or service is relevant you can differentiate your offer. The downside is if the niche is too narrow or there are already some strong competitors in it.

Penetration

Moving into new segments, or gaining a stronger presence in one. This approach might be used when you want to expand your market or make inroads against a competitor. You need to have the right sales people, pricing and sales structure.

Profit

A sales strategy which focuses on profit makes sense, although it might have an impact on volumes. The sales case needs to be compelling and the skills to deliver it strong. In a market where some competitors may be buying business you need to be sure of your position and willing to hold it.

Growth

This differs from volume because you are looking for more sustainable business. It is not only about getting more revenue it is looking to find growth either through more customers or by selling more to the customers you have. It requires good planning to identify or create the opportunities.

Key accounts

A sales strategy used by many organisations these days. This presents a number of challenges from identifying the target accounts (not necessarily the largest), setting up the right sales operation and making sure the internal functions are aware of the accounts and the implications for how they support sales.

Vertical

This can be a larger version of niche. A vertical strategy is usually chosen to serve a specific industry or market where you have relevant expertise through your product or sales people. Another benefit is that you can usually identify prospective customers and communicate with them more easily than in broad segments.

Retention

A valid sales strategy which is often overlooked. Having worked hard to win customers, it makes commercial sense to pay attention to keep them. This might mean that more attention has to be paid to customer service and support and that sales people keep in contact to retain and develop the relationships.

Market share

Setting your sales strategy towards gaining or maintaining market share is usually about getting a certain level of business. If you have an idea of the potential market size you can readily assess that the target market share will give you a certain level of revenue. Additionally, you can probably work out the potential costs and margins you can achieve and sustain. It also helps you focus on which competitors you need to take on and how to sell against them.

Margin

Rather than focusing on profit as the monetary amount, a margin strategy encourages the sales people to think about what they are selling and at what price. This gives them some flexibility within each deal across several sales providing they can achieve the target margin overall. It provides a good balance rather than pursuing volumes and discounting too heavily.

When deciding on your strategy consider the market segmentation targets, what is your value position for these segments and what sales process you will use to deliver the results. Be aware of any changes in your customer need, the competitors' activities, the environment, your own organisation's offering or strategy and revisit your sales strategy and adapt it if necessary.

The sales manager's checklist

■ Define the specific segments you want to target for sales activity, making sure they are relevant to the organisation's strategy.

■ Decide on the key strategic aims of your sales approach, assessing the potential benefits of them and also evaluating the challenges or any risks.

■ Communicate the sales strategy with the other functions of your organisation and be clear about what you need from them to support the sales effort.

■ Review the strategy and direction quarterly, considering the market, your customers and competitors and noting the possible impact of any changes.

Identifying your sales structure

Objectives

- To understand the different options for structuring your sales operation
- To identify the most effective structure for your sales strategy
- To assess the implications for other functions

Understanding

Many organisations create a sales operation and structure and then stick with it for years without really questioning whether it is the most effective approach for what is currently happening with their market and customers. I am not suggesting that the sales approach should be constantly changing, but it does need to adapt to be fit for purpose. A number of factors will need to be considered when thinking about your sales structure.

Internal	External
Company structure and strategy	Number of potential customers
Sales strategy and plans	Location of customers
Resources available	Complexity of sale
Sales process	Competitors' strategy
Company targets and objectives	Type of customer and their expectation

Your sales structure needs to be right for the type of product or service you are offering and where your organisation is in its own life cycle. If you have decided to use a field-based sales team you need to think about numbers and your sales cycle. Whether you start with sales people working on set geographical territories or working by vertical or product sectors will depend on the complexity of what you are selling and how technical or specialised is the knowledge needed. Generally, the geographical split is the easier start. However, you need to be aware how far you want the sales force to work from the centre so that you can deliver a good level of service at a reasonable cost to the business. At the same time, check that there are enough potential customers within each territory. Does your market use a transactional sales approach, or a more relationship or consultative one? Will your sales people have to keep prospecting and finding opportunities or do they need repeat visits and time to build relationships to grow more business from customers?

What needs to be included in the role and responsibilities of the sales people? How much of their time needs to be spent on areas such as marketing, lead finding, research, administration, financial elements, organising events and various ancillary and support tasks? If they have to be involved with any of these, what impact does it have on their available selling time? Can these be carried out by someone else?

When looking at the field sales option you need to think about the management structure too. Who is going to be responsible for the sales operation? Are they going to be able to give it the right level of attention and the people the right support? Your market and organisation's size will influence what you can do. Ideally, a sales director or senior manager will have two to eight direct reports and they may have several people under them in turn.

If you think that your organisation will be better suited by using telesales, you have a different set of factors to consider. (This does not have to be mutually exclusive from having a field sales operation. There are markets where the two can fit together very effectively.) The set-up of a telesales operation presents its own challenges. Identifying how many people you need is the first step because they can obviously handle more prospects and customers than territory sales people. You can mirror the field sales structure in terms of geographical split or by specific markets. Although some organisations keep in-bound and out-bound sales teams separate, this is not essential, especially if you are working with a small team.

The telesales team can have a similar management structure, although it is common to have team leaders or supervisors who provide the day-to-day support and direction. If telesales and field sales are being used in tandem, be clear about specific responsibilities and communication lines between the two. It is important to avoid duplicating activity and confusing or irritating customers.

A few years ago I was involved with a consultancy project where we were asked to look at the sales structure and operation and suggest improvements across the different divisions of a large company. Their main division had (in theory) over 140 sales people on their headcount. This presented its own challenges as they were usually 20–30 short of this. To make it worse, each territory had over 600 accounts, many of which were very small and were only contacted when contracts needed renewing. At the same time, 10–20% of their accounts produced over 80% of the revenue. To cut to the end of the tale, we recommended reducing the territory sales numbers to around 60 and to set up a telesales operation of about 12–15 people to handle the huge number of small accounts. The end result, overheads went down by about £¾m and sales volumes stayed the same for the first year and increased by 7–8% the following year.

Another option is to use other organisations to sell for you. This could be through specialist distributors, wholesalers or resellers. Many of these organisations will have their own sales forces and provide coverage of their local areas. You need to sell to their managers and sales people so that your products are promoted. This type of selling or distribution management is a skill set in itself. Your organisation may need to provide product training, and possibly sales training, plus appropriate technical and marketing support. There is also scope to sell through individuals who operate as sales agents. Many of the same principles apply and the challenge is to keep your product high on the agent's priority list rather than just something else in their portfolio.

Doing

When deciding on your sales structure, assess your business and intentions against the following factors.

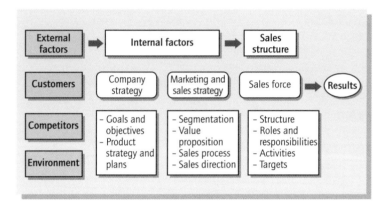

In the early stages of a sales organisation the role of the actual sellers is very important. They need to start to open up the market, creating awareness and generating business. You need to invest in and support them. Generally, to get some sort of momentum you will be better to have your own direct sellers rather than using distributors or any sort of reseller. You will have more control and influence over the direction. Alternatively, you could combine the two channels if you want to get a geographical spread without too much financial commitment to a larger number of sales people.

As you get more established in the market you need to do something to maintain and grow your position. This will require a larger sales presence and possibly more knowledgeable and specialised people. Although many people predicted that the growth in the internet would lead to the death of sales forces, the opposite has happened. What it has done is given prospective customers a greater ability to have more awareness of products and options. They want to deal with someone who can handle their questions and explain how the product or service will work. This is especially true in B2B markets and the sellers need to be able to talk about their offering in commercial and business terms. Whether the sales people are dealing with the prospects face to face or over the telephone, the concept is the same.

Moving through the life cycle to a mature stage and then on to decline, the dynamics change again. The size of the sales force may reduce and you might choose different channels with a move to resellers. The key is to maintain the existing and profitable relationships and be as efficient as possible. There is a decreasing need for technical expertise, although a decent level of product knowledge and application is still helpful.

When looking at the options for your sales structure keep checking where you are against the diagram above and overlay this with where your product is in the stages of the product life cycle (Introduction → Growth → Maturity → Decline).

At each stage the role of the seller changes to fit with the type of customer.

	Introduction	Growth	Maturity	Decline
Type of purchaser	Early adopters	Early majority	Followers	Traditionalists
Sales approach	Educate	Inform	Compete	Remind
Strategy	Penetrate	Market development	Product development	Maintain
Specialisation	Low–medium	High	Medium	Medium–low

Moving through these stages requires a change in the role of the sales people and also raises questions about the degree of specialisation they need and whether you change the structure to suit or train them to adapt. Do they need to become more market oriented and expert, or to develop more product and application knowledge? Is it relevant to change towards a key account strategy at one level, with a territory or distributor strategy to underpin this? How do the sales people direct their efforts and activities in their sectors? All of these elements need to be considered, and evaluated regularly, to be fit for the market and deliver the desired results in terms of performance, revenue and profit.

The sales manager's checklist

■ Look at how other organisations in your sector structure their sales operation. Can you learn from what they do and how they approach the market? What can you do differently?

■ Think about the different options for structuring your sales and assess the strengths and weaknesses of each.

■ Make sure your sales structure is right for your sales strategy and direction.

■ Revisit your sales structure regularly and check whether it needs adapting to suit any changes in the market or with your customers, or to reflect your own organisation's strategy.

■ Take care not to stick with a sales structure because 'that is the way we have always done it'.

The cost effectiveness of your sales function

Objectives

- To understand the costs involved in making a sale
- To know what to consider when looking at the real costs of your sales function
- To recognise the need to know the cost of recruiting and developing sales people
- To recognise the real cost of having underperforming sales people

Understanding

Have you any idea of the cost of each sales visit or sales contact made for your organisation? I suggest it is probably a lot more than you think. Various pieces of research indicate that a face-to-face meeting is likely to be somewhere between £250 and £400 (depending on your sector, it can be even higher in more complex or technical markets). How many meetings are needed to get an order? Many industries have an average of four to five meetings which gives you a substantial cost of sale. At the same time, the costs of an inside call are between £25 and £75. These continue to rise year on year and are a key factor for you to understand when analysing your sales direction and strategy.

Although sales is the essential function for an organisation because it generates the revenue, it can also be a very expensive area of the business, especially if any element is not functioning effectively. If you are a start-up business or introducing a sales operation it can be a daunting exercise to plan and implement one.

Your sales plan should include an outline for your sales operation, whether starting with just one person or looking at the wider sales force. Initially, setting the budget for the sales function might seem to be straightforward. Numbers of people, salaries, probable expenses, company benefits and contribution to overheads should be easy to calculate. However, when thinking about your sales costs it is worth considering more than the actual sellers and what you need to have in place to free them up to focus on their role. Can you ensure that there is the right support, administration and customer service infrastructure? If you are not able to do this, it adds to the costs exponentially because these activities take the sellers away from what you want them to be doing: contacting and dealing with prospects and customers.

Even when apparently freed to concentrate on their key result areas, it is worth breaking down how little actual sales time many sellers actually have. Look at some numbers and map them across to your own organisation.

Start with 365 days for the year and take away 104 days for weekends and 25 days for holidays plus 8 days for public holidays. (Some countries offer more than this.) We are down to 228 available selling days. Now consider monthly sales meetings: we are at 216 days. Anything to add for training, attending exhibitions or conferences, or possible sick days? Does your organisation expect the sellers to be in the office for any administration or planning or ad hoc activities? We are probably down to something between 180 and 200 days for selling and it could be a lot less.

Research from CSO Insights, in their 2012 Sales Performance Optimisation Survey, found that sales people were spending 37% of their time on selling activity with actual customer contact either face to face or on the telephone. This figure is down from 41.7% the year before. Initially, this is not necessarily all bad because some of the time change is being spent on market and customer research, although there is a downside with an increase in time being spent on post-sale administration and problem solving. If we take this into actual hours, it infers that most field sales people will be spending two to three hours a day doing what you really pay them for. The trick is to set up your organisation, structure, systems, support and processes to maximise the opportunities for your sales people to sell.

Doing

When considering the cost effectiveness of your sales function you need to weigh up a number of factors. Looking at existing sales people, how many are actually achieving their targets or quotas? In most sales organisations, this will be less than 60%, so the underperformers are a significant additional cost.

What impact do underperforming sellers have on your organisation and your sales plan? How long do you tolerate them for? Remember, an underperforming member of the sales force will incur a similar direct cost to one who is achieving their quota. They will drag down the overall performance and measures for effectiveness. Where they can cost more is in the indirect or hidden costs.

- Assess how much extra time they take from management and others in reviews, coaching and other interventions. (What could this time contribute if spent with the middle of the road and high performers?) They are often high maintenance.

- What are the customer costs and risks? Lost deals, lost revenue against target are obvious. How might they impact the customers' impression of your organisation or their satisfaction levels?

- Another area which can be affected is the internal staff and possible extra workloads or problems generated for them. There can be a creeping influence on morale amongst the sales colleagues and support staff.

The message is simple; do not tolerate underperformers for too long. Not only do they have a negative impact on your figures, it will take time to find a replacement and for them to become productive.

Understanding the cost effectiveness of your sales function starts with knowing the overall cost of recruiting a new seller. Let us look at some figures presuming an initial salary of £30,000 plus benefits.

Direct costs

Advertising and recruitment agency = £5K

Management and administration time for reading CVs, interviewing etc. (3 days) = £2K

Travel, logistics costs = £1K

Initial salary and benefit costs (4 months until productive plus work cover) = £12K

Formal training or induction = £2K

Sales lost whilst learning = £30K

Potentially you are looking at a direct cost of £52K to bring in a new recruit and get them up to speed where they can work on their own.

Then add:

Hidden or indirect costs

Cost of training and developing through coaching etc. (add opportunity cost for manager or coach being off their job) – possibly 40 hours = ??

Lost sales due to vacant territory (maybe 2 months to recruit, 1 month starting, then 3 months at 50% before productive) = 6 months of sales target

Customer loyalty and drift = ??

Team morale = ??

This is a significant investment and it will take time to find out whether it is a good one. You need to be aware of these because if you make a wrong choice you must act quickly. Do not hang on hoping against hope that someone will come good. Remember, the underperformer will be costing you even more than those who are delivering.

Now that you have your sales people, how cost effective are they?

> What do your sales people cost your organisation?
>
> Salary plus commission or bonuses = £40K
>
> Overheads, contribution and benefits, perhaps 20% of earnings = £8K
>
> Direct costs and expenses (will vary according to territory and market) = £18K for example.

These figures tell us that the sales person is costing £66K. Let us work on them having 180 selling days a year. They are costing you £366 per day. This is about £50 per hour. How many customer visits do they make on average each day? If they are only seeing one or two you can see why it is such a high cost per visit – and that does not count days when they do not make any.

What activities are they having to do which distract from customer research, contact and meetings? How can their sales contacts and calls be made more effective and productive? Before hiring more sales people can you enable them by identifying the tasks they are doing which are taking them away from their core role and bring in others to do those tasks? Surely administration support at £15 per hour is more cost effective than a £50 per hour sales person?

You can do a similar activity to evaluate the effectiveness of an internal sales operation, looking at possibilities for both out-bound and in-bound calls. Certainly your costs will be less than £66K per seller, possibly half that figure or even less. The cost per call or contact will be significantly lower as telephone sales will usually have many more calls per day. If you plan to use both internal and external sales teams can you have your inside sellers doing more to help to qualify opportunities and move things on with customers.

Check that your systems and processes are fit for purpose. That means that they are helping your sellers do their job and not just in place for internal operations or because they have always been there. Also, invest in and use the best technology to help research, prospect and customer contact, and for sharing customer information. If you are in a market which has products or services with any complexity, make sure your sales people are properly prepared for meetings. Research from Forrester Inc. showed that purchasers in technical markets found well over 50% were either unprepared or underprepared and only 13% were properly ready for meetings.

The sales manager's checklist

- Work out the cost of your sales function and sales people to fully understand what is involved.

- Understand the real cost of sale contact and calls, both for internal and external calls.

- Identify ways to improve efficiency and effectiveness of your sales team, whether helping them to make more calls or to be more productive in those calls.

- Communicate the costs with your sales people to help them understand the implications of any inefficiencies.

- Do not put up with underperforming sales people for too long. They are a significant cost and a drain on resources.

- Make sure your sales people are spending their time on activities which generate opportunities.

Interactions with other functions

Objectives

- To recognise the importance of developing and maintaining good relationships with other functions in your organisation
- To be a good role model in interactions with other functions
- To create a more collaborative approach to working across your organisation

Understanding

How do the various functions of your organisation view the sales function and the sales people? Do the managers and staff within them really understand what has to happen to get sales? Are they fully supportive of the sales people and activities? If you can give positive answers to these questions you are in a fortunate minority in my experience. Too many organisations operate with a silo mentality, with the focus on what is happening within their own function and little attention to anything beyond. This can lead to you feeling as though you are dealing with competition internally as well as your actual competitors. I mentioned the need to have a fit between different parts of the business to get alignment in strategy and plans. Whilst this is essential it is also important to have good working relationships between the different functions.

Sales is a challenging enough role without having to keep struggling with your own internal functions to have their support. Why does this seem to be the case in so many organisations? In many respects, sales people can be their own worst enemies in creating or perpetuating this situation. There are many stereotypes about sales and sales people and it seems to be hard or impossible to shift these. Rather than keep working at changing people's perceptions it seems to be easier to live up to them.

The sales operation impacts on every area of the organisation, directly or indirectly, not only because they all need sales to get orders and bring in revenue. As the leader of sales you have a vital role in facilitating the interactions between your operation and all of the others. There are several things you can do to help to improve the relationships for yourself and your people, starting with making sure you are a good role model for all. Adopt an attitude of collaboration. It is recognised that a key approach for sales success these days is collaborating, internally and externally, rather than competing.

You cannot make someone else collaborate; it might take time and they need to believe that it will be a better way to work. As an initial move, be clear and open in your communication with your colleagues. Encourage your sales people to do the same too. To enhance interactions with other functions develop your understanding of what they do, how they do it and why. I suggest you do this before expecting them to understand your function and the impact they have on what you are doing and where it might be unhelpful or even obstructive.

Although the quality of personal relationships and communication are important, the systems and processes are critical too. How well aligned are these? Are they working towards the organisation's strategy or just to the function's goals?

I was asked by a client to go in and run a workshop for the management team to align what they were doing. My contact said, 'We have been really good at getting the various quality and ISO certificates as an organisation, but it seems each department is focusing on its own processes and aims and not thinking about the impact on others or the overall business. Can you help us do something to improve this?' I went in and facilitated a workshop which started with a 'no blame' contract so that everyone could be open about what they were doing, what they expected and needed from each other, and what was the impact of how things were being done. We looked at the inputs, processes and outputs for each department. It proved challenging, stimulating and enlightening. A number of changes were agreed and implemented, communication improved and over the next three to six months so did the business performance.

Whilst looking at the impact of the other functions on sales, ask yourself (and their managers), what could your people do differently to help them? Are you sensitive to the other functions' needs and pressures or just concerned with what you want? How reasonable are the sellers in their requests or demands?

Doing

Take time to assess the range of interactions you, and your sales people, need to have. Identify those which seem to be effective and those where improvements can be made. Do this from your own perspective initially, and then in discussion with the sellers. Look at these from both formal and informal interactions and also your side and the other functions'. As you check this, think about whether any patterns emerge and what lessons you can take from these.

Look to what you want from the interactions with the other functions; define what you would like to achieve objectively in specific terms such as information, actions and timescales. Additionally, what would you like to get more subjectively from the relationships and behaviours? To reinforce things, involve the other functions and your colleagues to establish what they want so that it is not just a one-way process.

To help understanding of the other functions, spend some time with them. For you as the leader, spend time talking with your colleague and also with the staff in that function. Look at what they have to do, what their challenges are and how these influence their interactions with your function. At the same time ask for their input about what impact the sales people have on their work and how this affects the quality of what they can do for you. Do the same for all of the sales people, making them spend time in these functions and shadow the people for a time. If it helps their understanding and they empathise better with their colleagues, it can only help. For newcomers, make this part of the induction programme. To really enhance the interactions, it can be very useful to reverse this process and encourage the people in the other functions to spend time with the sellers (whether internally based or out in the field). This can dramatically change their perception of the sales role and what the people have to do. It can also help to develop an understanding of how their job and what they do can impact the customer. Everyone's job has some influence on the customer and their perception of your organisation.

When interacting in a more formal situation, such as a management meeting, remember to approach with a spirit of collaboration. The aim is to work together making life easier for your people and improving sales results. Be open to listening to observations about what is happening (or not) with your people. When discussing these issues or concerns you have, focus on understanding the reasons behind them and looking for solutions. In general, a 'How can we ...' approach is better than any implication of blame.

A method which some organisations use to improve their internal interactions is to create Service Level Agreements (SLAs) between each function. This is especially true in larger companies, but does not have to be limited to them. SLAs are often used between customers and suppliers when there is some element of ongoing service or delivery commitment. One of the principles for creating an SLA is that it provides a degree of clarity of what can be expected and what needs to be delivered. It is not intended to apportion blame but to provide the 'supplier' of the service with an awareness of what standards they need to work to and provide. At the same time, the 'customer' knows what they can expect in terms of response, both what and when. A good SLA is written both ways so that each side has to take ownership for their inputs to the other and for the outputs they deliver.

For the more subjective element of the interactions, be willing to work at improving the relationships and communication where necessary. Even where the other people might have very different personalities or styles of working, it is important that you develop the flexibility and interpersonal skills to work with them. You do not have to become personal friends. A professional, working relationship will do with a degree of rapport and respect. Keep in mind that your objective is to enable your functions to work well together and make it easier for your sales people and the other staff to do their jobs effectively.

The sales manager's checklist

▓ Talk to your team about how effective they find the other functions and identify what needs to be done to improve things.

▓ Introduce a process and a plan for you, your team and the other functions to improve their understanding of each other's roles.

▓ Make sure you adopt a collaborative approach to working with other functions, with a spirit of sharing and joint problem-solving.

▓ Be flexible when interacting with colleagues who are different in style and approach.

▓ Be a role model for collaboration and demonstrating constructive working with other functions.

▓ Recognise that some issues might be generated from the sales people and how they are communicating.

▓ Consider introducing Service Level Agreements between sales and the other functions you interact with.

part five

Managing the sales operation

Setting goals for your sales people

Objectives

- To understand the importance of setting clear objectives to provide a clear direction for your sales people
- To identify areas to set objectives rather than just revenue
- To use the SMARTER model for setting objectives with your sales people

Understanding

Most of us like our bosses to provide us with a clear sense of direction so that we know where we are going, and preferably why. Unfortunately, in many sales environments the sales force is just given some numbers to achieve, occasionally reinforced with messages about product mix or margins to achieve. Whilst these are important, they do not provide much direction or guidance, if any.

The foundation for what is covered in the sales direction comes from the sales strategy and sales plan, which was introduced in Part four. If you have done the plan it will give you some clear ideas about where you want your sellers to be going and what you want them to be doing. The concept is to direct them into activities which will deliver the revenue targets you require. Rather than thinking of your target as the objective, consider it to be the outcome of achieving your objectives.

If you only give your sellers a revenue target they will approach their job in different ways. Some might be organised and focused, others will be more reactive and inefficient, some may even panic or become quite negative and demoralised as they struggle to make any progress or overcome rejection from some of their prospects. Also, if the focus is just on targets, it makes meetings and reviews discussions about the numbers rather than what is producing them.

Making sure that your sales people have a clear sense of direction through effectively set objectives or goals is beneficial in several ways. Many models of motivation make the point that having goals and achieving them is a powerful motivator. You can focus activity into specific segments, accounts or product groups. You can adjust the direction to suit market changes. You can set different objectives for each seller so that they are relevant and at the right level for the individual.

You can provide direction by thinking about objectives in areas such as:

- New customers – numbers of, or different types of customer, new divisions within an existing customer.
- Product sales – specific products, product mix, introducing new products to customers.
- More contacts in existing customers – expanding DMU influence.
- Widening contact base between your organisation and customers.
- Particular projects.
- Customer or market information.
- Referrals or case studies.

Which could work for your organisation? What others can you think of adding?

Doing

Although setting the direction is ultimately the responsibility of the sales managers or leaders, this does not mean you have to do it in isolation. You can get other ideas by having conversations with colleagues such as marketing or customer service (where you have these functions) or the sales people themselves, especially the more experienced ones. Starting with the end in mind, the revenue target, work backwards to think about what needs to be done to reach it. Think of the end target as a finished house; work out the different elements which need to be completed to achieve it. Identify these component parts, timings and schedule and also 'dependencies', i.e. what has to be finished before another specific part is started.

When you have identified each area to set the objectives, think about how to make them clear and useful for each individual and you. A frequently used approach is to make sure your goals are SMART. Having said this, I do not believe it is used very well for a variety of reasons. I think you can be even more effective if you follow the idea of using SMARTER.

S – Specific: Check whether it is specific enough, with questions such as:

- What exactly do you want to achieve?

- Where do you need to go?

- Who do you need to see or develop a relationship with?

- Which products do you need to push?

M – Measurable: Can you put numbers to the objective? For the subjective or behavioural ones, ask 'How will you know when you have achieved it?' If this cannot be answered, it could suggest that the objective is not specific enough.

A – Achievable: (There are other versions, but I am sticking with this one.) This can be the tricky part to judge. The objective needs to be stretching enough to provide motivation and not too difficult so that people look and give up before they start. Equally, do not make it too simple because that has no real value if there is no sense of challenge. The other factor to think about is whether the objective is within the control of the individual. If not, is it fair to make them accountable?

R – Relevant: Does the objective relate to the individual's job and responsibilities? Does it fit with other objectives and, possibly, even support or reinforce them? Or, could it be pulling in a different direction?

T – Time bound: Most of us work better to deadlines, whether we like to admit it or not. Open-ended objectives run the risk of not getting finished or achieved.

A good way of setting goals is to have several working to different timescales: a good mix could be some short-term, maybe two or three months ahead; medium term over six months or a bit more; and long-term over nine months. As the short-term ones are finished, set others to replace them. This provides an ongoing momentum and will be more effective than just working to annual objectives and targets. Too many things can change in the market, with your customers, competitors or even within your own organisation, which can lead to the annual ones being irrelevant.

E – Evaluate: Once the objective is set, it is essential that you pay attention to how things are progressing. You need to evaluate performance and progress in order to support the individual or correct things quickly if they are slipping. (The action plan, which we cover below, will be a great help for this.)

R – Review: A real issue in many organisations, and not only with sales, is that people work diligently, achieve their objectives to a greater or lesser degree, and get no feedback or response from their managers. This step in the SMARTER model is really important for various reasons. It makes the whole process a learning and coaching activity, it acknowledges what is being done and achieved, and shows the individual that the manager is paying attention and involved. For both parties, lessons might be learned from how this objective went and how it can be applied in the future.

Working to this model can be a really good discipline. It encourages you, as a manager, to think about the areas in which to set goals and then pushes you into creating some form of process to make sure you are able to evaluate the progress towards each objective. Too many times objectives are vague and then nothing is done to monitor them. This devalues the whole exercise and leads to people not taking them seriously.

To really strengthen the power of objectives, and the likelihood of them being achieved, get your sales people to write them down (ideally following SMART). We develop a sense of greater commitment to something we have written rather than just talked about. To make the objectives even stronger, encourage your sales people to create an action plan for each one. Plans and objectives have little or no value without implementation. This is where action plans will help. There are many ways of doing them, and it is not important what method people use.

The key is to have an action plan for each objective. It will help the individual to achieve the objective and it will also help you to evaluate and monitor progress, managing and supporting them in the process.

My way of doing an action plan is simple. Draw a set of steps onto a blank sheet for each objective. Then work through identifying the steps you need to take towards achieving the objective and write them in. Put some 'marker' dates to keep you on track and to review progress. As a manager you need to put these in your own diary, to meet your seller and evaluate how they are getting along. The other two areas to note are any ideas for help or resources you need, as well as any possible problems and what you can do about them.

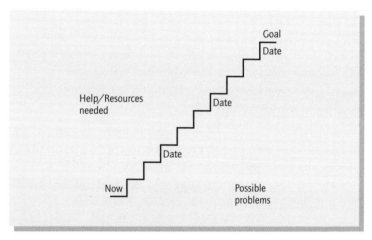

Remember, although you are responsible for identifying the area for the objective, it is going to be more valuable to have each sales person write out their own objective and their action plan. You get a copy of each, check over them to make sure they are clear, and then use them. These are your tools for the ER part of SMARTER. Do not blame your sales team if they are not clear about their objectives or what steps they need to take if you have not made them commit in writing. If you are not regularly meeting to discuss their action plans and evaluate progress and reviewing the objectives soon after the closing date, you are letting down both yourself and your sales people.

The sales manager's checklist

■ Treat objective setting, and evaluating and reviewing them, as 'A' priority tasks and do not allow other events to distract you.

■ Think about setting the direction as a different process to setting targets or quotas. This is the 'how' and "where', the targets are the 'what'.

■ Create a culture of objective setting within your sales operation and others where you can.

■ Let your sales people appreciate the value of having objectives and action plans by providing regular feedback on progress and praise for performance where appropriate.

■ Remember, having a sense of achievement and getting recognition of achievement (which can be as easy as 'Well done' or 'Good job') are powerful motivators.

■ Be a role model and let colleagues and sales people know your objectives, and make sure they are SMART. Share action plans, too, so that you demonstrate that they are more than a conversation topic and have value.

Identifying the right sales process

Objectives

- To recognise the benefits of having a sales process for all involved
- To be able to develop the right sales process for your organisation
- To understand how to break down the sales process into the right skills and behaviours at each step

Understanding

A number of people involved with sales feel that it is a free and easy area which depends on the style and personality of the seller and their adaptability for achieving results. This may be true some of the time, but it can be no coincidence that many large, successful sales organisations have identified their sales process and use it for developing and managing their sales people. They have recognised that it is not a good idea to allow their sales people to wander around without any clear plan or following best practice. It is accepted in many areas of business that there are processes which, when followed, help you achieve more efficiency and success. Why not do it in sales? As the quality guru Joseph Juran suggested in an interview in 1997, 'There should be no reason our familiar principles of quality and process engineering would not work in the sales process.' In fact he was late, because the Xerox Corporation had already identified and defined their sales process, which had the somewhat clumsy label of SPANCO (see later in this chapter).

What is a process? In principle, you will have inputs coming in, then various activities are carried out, which in turn produce outputs. To achieve the desired outputs both the inputs and the activities need to be 'right'. Any part which is not working towards the outputs is making it harder to achieve them.

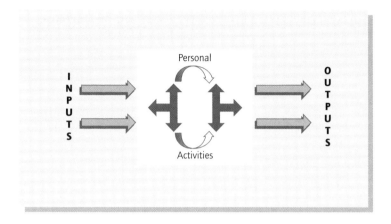

In Part one I talked about the sales funnel and pipeline. Your process should start at the beginning of this and lead through to winning the order and developing the account. Having a clearly defined process will help with keeping sales people focused and on track: either driving your sales methodology or fitting with it; identifying where there are development or training needs; forecasting sales; and monitoring and controlling the sales activity and people. However, there is little use in establishing your sales process if it is not embedded into the day-to-day work, and culture, of your sales function.

CSO Insights publish some interesting research in their annual sales management surveys and one element is around sales processes. They talk about four levels of sales process.

Level 1 they refer to as a random process. These are organisations which lack a process. Everyone does their own thing. They may be successful, some of the time, but will be unpredictable and unlikely to produce consistent results.

Level 2 might have an informal process. They may have a structured approach or process and expect people to follow it. However, it is not monitored or measured by management.

Level 3 organisations have a formal process. These companies will have defined a process and aim to enforce it, but their monitoring looks backwards and tends to be reactive.

Level 4 companies use a dynamic process. The process is an integral part of their sales, sales management and coaching. There is dynamic monitoring; the sales people get feedback on their use of the process. These companies will modify their process to meet changes in the market.

The reasons for using a sales process are compelling, especially when you look at the chart below.

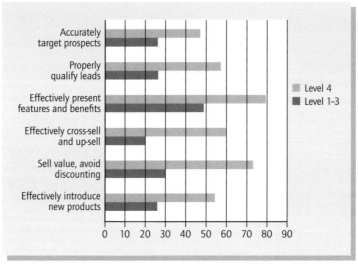

Source: © CSO Insights, LLC

If you use a sales process and treat it as Level 4, 20% more sales people achieve their quota (72% compared with 60% in Level 1 organisations) and forecasting is about 33% more accurate (58% compared with 44%).

Doing

If you look up sales process on the internet you might be overwhelmed by the 340 million references and the various claims to need anything between three and eight steps. I do not believe there is a 'right' number. The steps need to be right for your market and sales approach. I have worked with a client where a five-step process worked well and used the mnemonic PROBE and another which ended up with 12 steps. The latter

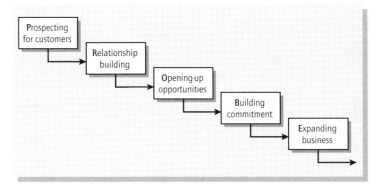

was rather extreme, although appropriate for the client who was selling complex IT solutions. The PROBE process was Prospecting customers, Relationship building, Opening-up opportunities, Building commitment, Expanding business.

There are several elements to consider when working on your sales process. Do not do it in isolation or just with an internal focus. An effective process will match the prospect's buying process and expectations. How well do you know these? Even before starting on your process, spend time identifying what happens in the prospect from the time when a need or want might be prompted or triggered, through to them making a buying decision. Although each prospect will have their own process, there will almost certainly be a number of similarities between them. This will give you a basis against which to consider the steps of your sales process.

The next stage is to start to assess your own sales process. One almost certainly exists, even though it has not been formalised or identified. It will have evolved as sales are made. If there is no formal process or sales model, each sales person develops their own way of working and when they find success they will repeat it, often without realising it. I believe that the most effective way of identifying the best sales process for your organisation is to use those who have been involved in sales and had some success. Get them to identify the things they do or did which worked. They will usually be able to come up with something similar to:

- Contact them in the right way
- You act professionally and confidently
- Treat *them* as individuals and get to know *them*
- Take an interest in *their* business
- *Listen* to *their* concerns and their business issues
- Give examples of how organisation can help and support them
- Make things relevant for them and their business
- Use a consultative approach showing knowledge
- Develop a feeling of confidence in organisation and what it can offer
- An approachable organisation
- A non-irritative approach
- You are responsive to their requests

Relationship building

- Build rapport – interpersonal skills
- Start to build trust in your professionalism
- Understand the person, their personal objectives and drivers, likes and dislikes
- Understand their business
- Get information about their business
- *Listen* to them
- Build trust
- Understand their hierarchy or structure
- Decision process: how – where – who – when
- Defining and checking the DMU
- Identify the decision criteria
- Commercial factors – spend, preferences of manufacturers, competitors
- Present branch overview
- Regular contact

Those who are working on this will identify the number of steps required. If you can find labels for each which can spell out a word, that can help to make it more memorable and embed it into the sales culture. However, this is not what makes the process so powerful. The detail is what matters. When working with clients I encourage them to identify what the prospect expects from the seller at each step and then look at the specific best practice behaviours which will match these.

The sales manager's checklist

- Look for examples of sales processes for other organisations in your market to see whether they might prompt your thinking.

- Understand the typical buying processes used by your customers and prospects, especially who is involved and when, before it arrives at the purchasing function or request for a proposal.

- Involve others in defining the key steps in your sales process. Note how these match the buying process and think about how to handle any areas where there might be gaps.

- Check these steps against what actually happens in the day-to-day sales activity.

- Break down the customers' expectations and your best practice activities at each step. Define these and write them down.

Using the sales process to deliver results

Objectives

- To be able to use the sales process to develop the skills of your sales people
- To understand how to use the process to improve sales forecasting
- To recognise how to use the process to review progress with prospects and against opportunities
- To know how to make your sales process into a Level 4, dynamic process

Understanding

The research shown in the previous chapter indicated that making your sales process an integral part of everything in the function will result in improvements in many areas of performance. To have a real Level 4 sales process requires genuine commitment from the organisation and its management, not just the sales leaders. I have worked with a number of clients who see the merit of having a sales process and develop and define theirs. The problem comes with embedding it into their sales culture. They find it too much of a challenge to move it from either informal (Level 2 – we have a process and think it's a good idea to use it but the real focus is on the numbers) or a formal process (Level 3 – we have the process, train people against it and it is built into our reporting but only checked against what has occurred) through to the dynamic Level 4. It has to be something which is used in all aspects of selling and sales management, and not optional, or nice to do if you feel like it.

To have a really effective, dynamic sales process which helps to deliver performance needs the sales people to fully understand the what, why and how of it. (So do the sales management if they are to manage the process.) Not only the main steps; also the specific best practice activities and behaviours. You can help this by printing the process and making sure everyone has a copy and, sometimes even more helpful, having a small laminated card with the main steps on one side and possibly some prompts or reminder questions on the other. If you can create a mnemonic such as PROBE, use it whenever you can to talk about sales progress. Providing the knowledge about the process and support material is important. To really get buy-in to it, make sure the sales people know why the process has been developed, and why they need to follow it. (A good process does not intend to produce clones or reduce individuality. It is about using what works in the same way as learning the principal steps to serve at tennis or to hit a golf shot.) In effect, they need to see the benefits and want to know, 'What's in it for me?' The how element can be covered through training, demonstrating and coaching.

If used effectively, the sales process underpins what the sellers actually do and it provides the organisation with the basis for setting targets and standards. A well-defined process will help with forecasting too. You can introduce some metrics based on which stage you have reached and what information you have uncovered. It can also help with assessing probability of opportunities which leads to more accurate forecasting, as mentioned in the previous chapter. There is also evidence that a good process will improve your conversion rate to achieve more sales, and enable you to have fewer 'no deal' situations, which helps to reduce wasted time.

The key to ensure you have a proper Level 4, dynamic process, is to revisit it regularly and evaluate how effective it is for the market. Neglecting this can lead to your sales process becoming unfit for purpose. Markets change, customers' situations move and competition is rarely static as they may change strategy or newcomers appear. Your process needs to be adjusted to accommodate any of these so that you can maintain, or even increase, your sales effectiveness and potentially enhance your competitive advantage.

Doing

Implementing an effective sales process has implications for many aspects of the organisation. When you know what is required for sales success it helps to shape the type of person who might be suitable for your market. The process indicates the skills and behaviours you want and these can be assessed at recruitment.

A clear definition of the skills and behaviours helps to identify what needs to be covered in your sales training. What specific areas require focus? The overall structure of any sales courses needs to fit with the process so that there is a likely synergy and not a risk of conflict through mixed messages.

Whatever your role, if you are working with someone involved with or responsible for selling, have conversations about where they are in the process with any prospect or customer. Take it into the detail of the behaviours, not just the step they have reached. At the same time, talk about how they are finding the buyer's expectation and whether they are meeting it. When making field visits, or any form of dual call, with the sales people keep the process in mind. Use it as a template to check how the seller is doing. Are they following it? How are they doing against the best practices? Encourage the sales people to assess themselves against the specific behaviours when reviewing the call.

Incorporate the sales process into your CRM system or whatever records you are using. The process can be broken into steps within steps if it helps to create the pipeline in a meaningful and manageable format. By embedding it into these systems the process can be used as part of the call planning and preparation and reporting. The sales people are expected to think where they are in the process and where they would hope or expect to be after the call. When completing their visit or call report they need to identify how they progressed against the plan and outline their objectives for moving to the next step. If this is monitored and managed by the management it becomes a habit.

Once you have your sales process and it is being used with some consistency, you can think about how to use it to improve your forecasting. There are two possible elements to this. The first is to establish the ratios which work for your organisation between each step. Thinking back to the original Xerox sales process of SPANCO, they used this to monitor progress and to improve their forecasting.

S - suspect = identifying people who 'may' be interested or have a possible use for the product.

P - prospect = those suspects who had a requirement and budget and would be in a position to make a decision within the agreed timeframe.

A - analyse = assess their specific situation, likely requirements, volumes, etc.

N - negotiate = discuss the requirements and negotiate to reach an agreement for what is needed.

C - close = ask for commitment to the order.

O - order = get the actual order, follow-up and develop the opportunity.

They were able to put numbers to this process at each stage. This provided them with data they could manage and coach against and, more importantly, forecast sales. Working backwards, for each order they could assess how many times they needed to close, and how many negotiations they needed, etc.

If the sales person needed two orders a week – they need to be closing three opportunities – which might mean six negotiations – nine analyses – and twelve prospects, and these come from thirty suspects. Everyone knew they needed to be identifying thirty suspects and qualifying twelve prospects each week. The sales process can provide you with these ratios. To be fair, in the 21st century sales arena things are a little different with the use of technology on both sides. However, the principle holds true.

As you move through each step, you are gathering more information and understanding of the prospect's situation. The further you move through the process, the better your chances of achieving an order, and the more accurately you can forecast or predict the outcome. Work with your sellers and assess the probability of getting the order at each step, or stages within them. At the prospect step it might be only 10%; by the time you are negotiating it might be 33% at the start and rise to 50% or more at the end. So, if your potential order is £1,000, you can forecast £500.

Use the process in the discussions in internal sales meetings to keep everyone focused on it and to show why it has to be integral to the business. If something has happened in the market, or the process has not been revisited for several months, take time to look at it again and in detail. Are the steps still relevant? What about the specific behaviours? Do these need adapting? How are the buyers changing in their expectations?

Make your sales process dynamic and insist on it being used by every sales person and all managers and it will repay you with more business.

The sales manager's checklist

- Make sure you believe in the principle of the sales process otherwise it will only become an exercise and be no more than a Level 2.

- Share the process with all other functions of your organisation.

- Incorporate the sales process into your CRM or record system.

- Use the process in conversations with your sales people, whether about potential sales meetings or reviewing progress.

- Regularly review and adapt your sales process to ensure it is appropriate for the market and what is happening or changing.

- Identify the measures for potential success for each step and within them to use to improve the accuracy of forecasting.

Establishing standards of performance

Objectives

- To understand the concept of standards of performance (or key performance indicators)
- To be able to identify areas to set the SOPs for your sales people
- To understand how to use standards to drive sales performance
- To set both quantitative and qualitative standards and share these with other functions

Understanding

A challenge for any manager or leader is to ensure that they are treating everyone fairly and sales is no exception. In fact, at times, it can be harder to achieve fairness in sales because so much of the judgement is based on sales results. Although achieving sales are an important measure there can be many factors which contribute to successes and management either can be blinded as to how the seller is working, or tolerates them because of their results. To improve the chances of treating people fairly, setting standards of performance or key performance indicators (SOPs or KPIs) can be very useful. I realise that organisations have their own preferred terminology but for this book I am sticking with standards of performance.

What are standards of performance? How do they differ from objectives or goals? My definition is, they are the various elements of behaviour and different activities which underpin performance. They are a baseline of expectation and will be the same across the operation. In principle, everyone has to operate to the same standards. There might be occasional exceptions such as when you have a new starter: you might set someone a lower standard and one of their goals can be to improve until they reach the desired level. Additionally, the standards do not have to be static. As the overall competence and experience develops, the bar can be raised to reflect this.

It is important that your people can see the purpose of the standards and not feel that they are just set for the sake of it. The standards need to relate to the key areas of the seller's job to help them understand their relevance. The detail of the sales process can provide some ideas for areas in which to set them, as well as your overall expectation of performance and behaviour. It is useful to explain the potential consequences for performance of not meeting the standards. If they become established they provide a sound foundation for your sales operation and help to create a good, professional culture. They will also be helpful when recruiting new sales people, because you can share the standards with applicants so that they know what will be expected of them. I also believe that many people like to work for organisations which have clear standards.

When setting standards you can have two types: quantitative and qualitative. As the names suggest, the former have numbers built into them and are easy to monitor and manage. The latter are less straightforward as they are subjective and more behaviourally oriented. Although the quantitative standards are easier to check, the ideal is to have a combination of the two types.

Doing

Setting standards of performance can be a challenge for many managers. Identifying the best, or most effective, areas in which to set them is the first hurdle. Having done this, establishing the right levels for them to provide a fair yet stretching baseline is essential. There are several ways of approaching these two tasks and you need to test them out to find which works best for you and your organisation.

If the concept is new to you, there is no harm in checking whether you can find any examples of standards being used by other organisations and their sales functions. You can use these as a starting point to give you ideas for areas in which to set standards and levels to aim for. If there are no immediate examples from competitors, look to other sectors and their sales functions. Benchmarking your own organisation against others is always a good basis to build upon and learn from. You may not be in a position to set yourselves at the same level as some others yet, but you can aspire to reach those. The important thing is to make a start.

If you have some experienced sales people, a good way to set standards and get buy-in at the same time is to involve them with the process. You can also get input from other departments within your organisation, especially on areas which might affect them.

Working with an internal sales and support team on a workshop about 'Delivering Service Excellence' we had an exercise on defining the SOPs for the function and the individuals. The syndicates presented their ideas back to the group and eventually an agreed list of activities, behaviours and measures was compiled. Later, when we broke for lunch we were joined by the top management team. They read the list with interest and asked how the items had been decided and by whom. When told the group had done it all, the management team commented that they agreed with everything listed but said they would not have dared to suggest some of the levels identified and defined in the measures. Although impressed, they were concerned these might be too much of a stretch. We checked that the group were happy with what they had set and believed they could achieve these. Three months later these standards were being met or exceeded and customer satisfaction was improving and complaints reduced by 30%.

Most sales markets still work as something of a 'numbers' game' despite changes in markets, with customer buying habits and the increasing use of technology. When identifying standards, you can set them to reflect the necessary numbers, especially in the early stages of the sales process. The qualitative standards can be tied in to some of these areas and also applied for the behaviours required for selling, interacting with others and dealing with the administrative tasks.

Examples of quantitative standards:

- To contact ten suspects per week.
- To make five customer visits per week.
- To respond to customer messages or enquiries within six hours.
- To produce initial reports with a maximum of two errors.

Examples of qualitative standards:

- To complete customer records accurately and fully each day.
- To be able to identify where you are in the sales process for each customer and prospect.
- To maintain your company vehicle in a clean and tidy state.
- To communicate openly with colleagues, ensuring they have all relevant information.
- To be able to present (or demonstrate) your products fluently and confidently.

When establishing your standards they can be more powerful if they are:

- *Relevant* – people need to see how these fit with their job, objectives and the sales direction.
- *Clear* – everyone can understand what is expected.
- *Fair* – everyone knows they have to work to the same standard.
- *Adaptable* – they can be moved up or down or reframed if people are struggling to meet them, or exceeding the original levels set.
- *Respected* – credit is given when levels are met. They are not moved or raised without some discussion.

(To be fair to you, it will take some time and experience to be able to achieve all five of these consistently.)

The sales manager's checklist

▓ Identify some organisations that you would like to benchmark your sales operation against.

▓ List specific areas or items where you want to set standards and decide which can be quantitative and which qualitative.

▓ Liaise with other functions for their input on standards and how you can use them to benefit everyone.

▓ Use your sales people to get their input into both areas for standards and levels to set.

▓ Where you have set the standards for your sales people, communicate them clearly and make sure they understand and buy into them.

▓ Publish and share the standards with your sales people and the other departments in the organisation.

▓ Revisit the standards and discuss their adherence and relevance. Be open to adjusting them to suit.

▓ Use the standards consistently across your sales people when assessing or reviewing performance.

The monitoring and control system

Objectives

- To understand the importance of having a clear and effective control system
- To know how to use the control system to monitor the sales activity and performance
- To be able to develop an appropriate sales control system for your organisation

Understanding

Many people leading sales functions spend too much time focusing on the sales results. I am always mystified by this, especially those organisations where I see senior managers getting daily information about sales and making calls to those responsible, demanding their thoughts or justifications for that day's or week's figures. What do they expect to happen or to change and how quickly? This is even more puzzling if they are in a market where the sales lead time (from meeting the prospect through to order) is weeks or months. It is a bit late to be panicking.

The issue is that they are dealing with the symptom – not the cause. Yes, there are reasons for the lack of sales but looking for them when assessing the results is not going to identify the cause. In fact, the reasons which might be given may not be an accurate reflection of the real problems. Another issue is that even if the cause is identified, how long will any corrective action take to produce results?

This situation arises because the organisation either does not have an effective monitoring and control system, or it does not use the one it has properly. Either members of management do not pay enough attention to it as a monitoring tool or they do not insist on their sales people using it. Many sales people do not enjoy filling in plans or reports, perhaps because they think of them as a distraction from their selling activity or they see no value in doing so. This is frequently because management does not communicate the purpose of the reports or system or provide no feedback on what is done. It can also be because the system being used is too unfriendly.

The simplest and yet effective way of setting up a good monitoring and control system in my experience is to have a 'before' and 'after' element. Whether this is run through a full CRM system or a paper-based one does not matter, the principles still apply. The 'before' step requires the seller to complete a form outlining what they are doing in the coming week or weeks, who they are planning to visit, call, e-mail, etc., and what the objective is for each. This needs to be sent to you before the start of the time period being covered. The 'after' part is a report of where they have been, who they saw, what was achieved or agreed and what is planned next – and when. If you want to monitor types of call or call mix, this can be included, and even products covered.

The sales people need to understand why this needs to be implemented and how you will use it. A really effective monitoring and control system will be easy to complete for the sellers. It will be even more productive if they can see how using it can help with their own planning and assessing how they are performing. If they understand how their SOPs can be tied in with the system, they are likely to be even more inclined to use it properly. The thing you want to avoid is where sales people are filling in half truths or fudging it to make it look as though they are doing the right things. A good system will enable you to spot if this is happening. If you are introducing a system to sales people who have not had to use one before, do not have any concerns about arguments around trust. It is not that you distrust people, but your sales people are a highly expensive resource. Surely, it is a responsible action to be monitoring what the resource is doing? The only sales people who should have any concerns are those who are not doing their jobs honestly. Completing the plans and reports is not a negotiable part of the job; everyone has to do them – properly.

Doing

In the same way as you need an effective sales process to deliver the results, you need a monitoring system which works with the process. Just having something which reports results is of limited value, if any.

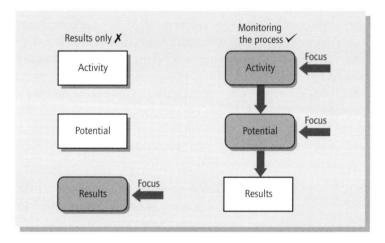

The results are an outcome of the right level of activity being directed into the right potential contacts. If the results are not what you need, to examine the issue, start earlier in the process. Why wait until you see the results? Redirect your attention to the activity levels initially.

Introduce the concept of the before and after elements of the system. Create a simple, yet clear format for the forward plan. I believe it should be something similar to this:

Date	Organisation	Contact	Type of call	Step in sales process	Objective

When managing sales people, I was always interested in knowing where they planned to go and why. If they were not clear about this I considered it as an early warning sign that they may be struggling to achieve the right activity level. This plan would also indicate whether they were seeing people with the right potential.

Many organisations already have some sort of sales report or call report. I believe that these need to be designed in a way which enables them to be completed reasonably quickly whilst providing useful information. In their simplest format they could duplicate the columns of the pre-call form, with two additional ones showing whether the objective was achieved, and next steps. You need to think about what you need to have reported and be able to monitor. The aim is to check where things are in the sales process and whether the activity and potential areas are on track. Avoid asking for too much information or detail. Some might do it for you, many will not. I have worked with organisations which want lengthy written reports of sales visits. My concern is what real value these add to the process, the sales person or the management? Are they even read?

It is important that you actually use the information you are receiving from the system. If you are not monitoring things in the early stages, the activity into the potential, how can you forecast results? The system will indicate whether the sellers are achieving the right activity levels. However, if they are doing this and struggling with results, is the problem with the people or organisations they are contacting, the potential not there? If, on analysis, they seem to be making the right volume of contacts to the right potential, is the problem with their selling skills? The monitoring and control system does not always tell you the problem; it does indicate where it might be occurring and what questions to ask.

You can encourage a better degree of commitment from your sales people by communicating the reasons for introducing and using the system and how you will utilise it to help them. Once people have started using it, make sure you talk with them about what they are planning and have done. When meeting with your sellers, use their plans and reports as a key part of your discussions. You can use these to give positive feedback where appropriate and also pick up whether there are any trends or mismatches between what they planned to do and what they are reporting from what they actually did.

The sales manager's checklist

- Aim for the three elements for your monitoring and control system – plans for before, reports after and customer records.

- Make sure you move your focus from monitoring results to looking at the inputs (activity and potential).

- Create a simple weekly or monthly planner and share this with the sellers. Be open to slight changes using their input, but not moving away from the concept. Design a suitable call or activity report to give you the information you want.

- For all aspects of your monitoring and control system, identify what is 'must have' and 'nice to have' in each step.

- If you are using an IT-based CRM, integrate this into it, presuming there is not something already available within it.

- Incorporate your SOPs into the plans and reports where you can or make sure they provide information to monitor those.

- If something is not fitting with expectations at the early stages, step in early to make the corrections. It will require less effort to make the changes here than when results are being missed.

- Insist on the plans and reports reaching you on time and properly completed.

Managing sales people

Recruiting the right sales people

Objectives

- To recognise the challenges involved with recruiting the right sales people for your organisation
- To understand the need for job descriptions and personal profiles for the positions
- To approach recruitment in a structured and professional way

Understanding

Finding and keeping good sales people is a challenge for most organisations. As mentioned in 'The cost effectiveness of the sales function' in Part four, the cost of a new recruit can be over £50K before they become productive, plus other potential hidden costs. This is a considerable investment for any organisation and you want to get it right more often than getting it wrong. The cost of getting it wrong rises frighteningly with further lost revenue, damage to customer credibility, negative impact on other internal people and absorption of your time.

Sales recruitment has additional pressures compared with other positions. The need to have someone covering the sales territory as soon as possible is an ever-present concern because of worries about losing business and customer relationships and trust. This can be even worse if someone has left and joined a competitor (or started up on their own) and is covering the same area. Another problem is how the territory will be covered whilst filling the vacancy? Do you have to do it yourself? Spread it between other sellers, if you have them? Do you only respond to enquiries or does someone actually continue with customer visits? These issues, in combination, can lead to the making of some rushed and poor decisions when taking on sales people.

A significant contributor to the challenges involved is that most managers, and many of you reading this, have probably had no real training in the whole recruitment and selection process. I find it a mystery why organisations should presume that, when someone is given a role where they are involved with recruitment and selection, they are sprinkled with some sort of magic dust providing them with the necessary expertise. Even stranger when you think that they are possibly investing in a resource costing over £50K. Not every organisation has a Human Resources function to help with the process. Even if they have, the line managers need to be involved at some stage.

Taking a structured approach will help you to realise that it is a lot better and more cost effective to concern yourself with getting it right rather than finding someone quickly, who may not be suitable once they start. If you are replacing a sales person who has left, check why they went. Was it their choice? Why did they go? (Exit interviews can be extremely valuable to understand whether there are things you need to improve in your organisation.) Is there any pattern for their territory or across the other sellers who leave? It makes sense to address this before bringing in someone new to face the same problems. Maybe it was your choice and you initiated their departure. Explore some additional aspects. What is the history of the territory? How are sales, and how have they been? Has it proved a problem for previous sales people? Also, take a step back and look at the person you recruited and whether you could have done anything differently? There is no point in repeating previous mistakes, so learn from what happened before.

The first step in the recruitment process is to establish reasons and background for the vacancy. Apart from aiming to avoid repeating mistakes, it can help to define what type of person you need to find to fill the position. If you are replacing an established seller and it is a strong, profitable sales territory you need someone different to the person who will fit into a territory which has had several people on it in the recent past and is struggling to deliver reasonable figures.

I do remember when starting out in sales on my first day out on my own getting a frequent message along the lines of, 'You must be the fourth one we've seen from your company this year' or words to that affect. Luckily, I was stubborn enough to decide that presented an opportunity for me and started to respond with, 'OK, so how many times do I need to keep calling before you will consider using my company rather than the competition?' This was usually delivered with a smile and got a range of humorous but encouraging responses. It probably helped that I was selling in London and the pace and type of interactions was different to a more rural territory.

An additional element many organisations use is psychometric testing or some form of personality assessment. These can be useful to give you additional information about the candidates which you can then explore during the interviews. Please do not get drawn into thinking that these can give you a totally accurate picture of an individual or tell you whether the candidate will succeed in sales. There will be some profiles which may struggle more than others, and some which would suggest a better likelihood of success. However, neither is guaranteed to be right. (Many of the models suggest that I should never have worked in sales or training, yet I haven't done too badly in both.)

Doing

I often think of the recruitment process as a series of steps.

1   Why has the vacancy occurred? (Work through the questions above.)

2   Do we need to replace the position exactly as it is? (Use the situation to reappraise your sales structure and set-up. Too many organisations just replace automatically, rather than taking it as an opportunity.)

3   Have we got a current job description and personal profile for the position? (If not, who will write them? It is difficult

to move through the next few steps effectively without them.)

4   Do we have anyone we can move into the position or do we know anyone? (Is this a chance for a development move for someone inside the organisation? Does anyone in the company know of a possible candidate? This might be a better option than going totally outside.)

5   How will we go about the recruiting process? Do our own advertising? In which media? Use some of the on-line jobsites? Handing the vacancy to a recruitment company or agency? Let the market know through social media, e.g. LinkedIn?

6   Who will write the advertisement or brief the recruiters?

7   How will we handle the applications? Who will do it? (Be prepared for dealing with large numbers, especially if advertising or using social media. Make sure you are set up to let *everyone* have an acknowledgement, even the unsuccessful applicants. Remember, this whole process is also about projecting a professional and favourable impression of your own organisation.)

8   Who will interview the applicants – for the initial interviews and a second or even a third meeting? (My suggestion is that you should have two interviewers at each step, ideally with the line manager as a constant. This gives you several opinions about the applicants and they may well appear different at each step.)

9   What is your timescale and schedule for interviews? (Bear in mind you need to read through applications properly and prepare for the interviews themselves.)

10   Have we prepared how we will approach the interviews? How will we assess the applicants?

Do you have any job descriptions? If you do, when were they last updated? If not, there are plenty of templates available on the internet. Aim to make them simple enough to be read quickly and clear about the job. In general terms, a job description will include:

- The overall objective or aim for the job
- The reporting line
- The key responsibilities and tasks
- The accountabilities of the role – some will also include 'permissions' or levels of authority.

The personal profile concentrates on the type of person and the characteristics they need to do the job. Take care when compiling this that you do not stray into falling foul of the law by including criteria which might be discriminatory. (There is a range of areas to avoid around gender, race and age, plus some others besides. Check because these change too.) When drawing this profile it can be specific for the sales territory and the character you believe you need to handle it. List what you want under two headings: 'Must have' – essential for the job; 'Nice to have' – useful if they have them.

The areas you might want to include could be:

- *Background and experience*: Do you want them to know your industry or sector? Do they need this knowledge or sales experience? If you want sales experience, check that they understand the fundamentals and will fit with your sales strategy. (Looking to take on someone from a competitor is not necessarily an ideal solution. Why would their good sellers want to move? Will their demands undermine your salary structure?)
- *Skills*: What do you need them to be able to do? What evidence will you need to see? How can you check these at the application stage and then at the interviews?
- *Personal qualities*: What do you want to see? From your knowledge of the job's key activities, tasks and responsibilities, what will the job holder need to be able to demonstrate in order to cope with these?
- *Education and qualifications*: What level do your sales people need to be able to do the job? Is a degree essential? Why? Do they need any technical education or professional qualifications?

Combining the job description with the personal profiles will give you the information necessary to draft your advertisement or briefing to the recruitment agency. Be really clear about the core responsibilities and the 'must have' factors for the job so that you can use these when evaluating applications.

When you have selected who you are going to interview, decide on your selection criteria. These should be written and shared with all who will be involved in the interviewing process. The selection criteria should:

- be written in terms of observable and measurable behaviours
- be based on an objective analysis of the job and its requirements
- specify the absolute minimum requirements needed to perform the job effectively
- be written to include skills, knowledge or experience that the person needs to have from day one of the job
- be written with a view to ensuring fairness and legal compliance in selection
- focus on competence as well as experience and track record.

You can now look through the applications for those you are going to interview and prepare your questions against the specification, those for the candidate and what information you need to give about the company.

Then follow the Seven Stages to Interview Structure:

1 Welcome and Introductions, give an outline for the process (or agenda)
2 Ask them to expand on their experience and achievements in present and recent job
3 Explore candidate's experience and achievements relative to the selection criteria
4 Supply information about your company and the job
5 Close the interview and tell them the next steps.
6 Assess against the selection criteria.

7 Review and discuss candidates with colleague and select short list or successful person.

The sales manager's checklist

▨ Use the ten steps as your initial checklist. Decide on what position you need to fill.

▨ Make sure you have current job descriptions and develop a personal profile for the specific vacancy.

▨ Be clear about the 'must have' criteria and why they are in this category.

▨ Define your selection criteria before starting any interviews and share them with the others involved.

▨ Do not play games at the interviews. Remember, recruiting is a two-way process where you are choosing from the candidates and they are deciding where they want to work. The power is not always with you; the good candidate may have it.

▨ Approach the interviews with a PROBE mindset – Prepare, Relax (all of you), Open up (get them talking), Balance (talking and listening), Explain (next steps).

Remuneration and rewards

Objectives

- To understand the different options for sales remuneration
- To recognise the benefits of ensuring the rewards are linked to the behaviours you want
- To understand the connection between remuneration and motivation

Understanding

Deciding on the best way to pay your sales people is an on-going challenge for most organisations. There is no single 'best' solution to this challenge. Even within well-rewarded sales forces there will be some who like the package on offer and others who will find something to complain about. Despite what you might think, money alone is not the ultimate driving factor for every successful sales person. You can always find some exceptions to this, claiming to be inspired by the money they can earn. Actually, the reality is they are driven by what the money helps them to buy, whether a bigger house, a boat or the Rolex watch. They like the sense of achievement in generating the income – and the recognition of their success through the material possession and the fact others can see it. Many more people, in sales jobs and other roles, are motivated by less materialistic factors.

There are many variables to consider when thinking about what remuneration package to offer your sales people (and sales managers). A key point to start from is to know what is provided in your market in overall terms. You need to be competitive in what you offer without necessarily being at the top of the scale. Offering the highest package but with poor support, products or management style will not get you the best sales people or, more importantly, keep them. You can often find this data with a bit of research. If you do use exit interviews to establish people's thoughts about your organisation when leaving, do not always believe the story that they are going somewhere else for more money. That is the easiest line to give you rather than telling you some truths about how they have been managed. It is a bit like a prospect or customer telling you that you are out on price rather than other reasons about your proposal or product.

The market will often influence how the package is made up, especially in terms of split between salary and commission. Or is the trend for a salary and bonus or even salary only? Some sectors still operate on a commission only basis. You do not necessarily have to follow your market exactly; you may prefer to go your own way. The other differentiator will be the country or countries you are operating in. There can be wide variations between what is typical.

In addition to the actual income package which is available, there are other elements which can be significant in the eyes of your sales people. Although many of these may not seem critical, not considering them can lead to demotivation. This can grow when sales people start talking to each other or have time on their own driving to calls and getting into a negative thought cycle about how hard done by they feel. I have known quite a few sales people leave their jobs because of a change in company policy about expenses, the smart phones they are provided with or the company cars. Often they go to organisations with inferior products or less supportive management just for the tangible extras.

Whether large or small, organisations need to pay close attention to their outgoings, especially in difficult economic times. Typically, they start with addressing a number of direct costs and impose restrictions in areas such as hotel bills, travel budgets, entertainment and even telephone use. Whilst both understandable and responsible business practice, some of these steps should be looked at as part of a bigger picture. Organisations can benefit from thinking about how these messages might be perceived and the possible impact on their sellers. I am not advocating unlimited expense accounts and use of 5-star hotels but there does need to be a balance. Organisations are often asking a lot from their sales people such as long hours, staying away from home, and a bit of give can compensate for the take.

Doing

The salary and benefits packages you offer can have an impact on performance. However, it is an area that the organisation and you, the manager, need to monitor. You need to make sure you are competitive in your marketplace and that your salary and reward structure is driving the behaviours you need. People will generally do what is inspected – and rewarded.

Looking at the standard options for reimbursing your sellers, there are advantages and disadvantages for each.

Type of pay	Advantages	Potential disadvantages
Salary only	Known fixed cost	Can lead to laziness
	Can create loyalty from sellers	Needs careful management
	Allows for longer sales cycle	Some sellers don't cover costs
Salary plus bonuses	Costs can be forecast	Salary might be enough for some
(e.g. salary + 10% against achievement of quota)	Costs are manageable	What happens to those who just miss quota?
	Good for building loyalty	Does not reward over-achievement
	Gives acknowledgement of success	
	Effective with long-term sales and account relationships	

▶

Type of pay	Advantages	Potential disadvantages
Salary plus commission (e.g. basic salary + commission on each sale or sales over quota. Might be 50% salary with 50%+ commission)	Gives some security through basic salary Rewards success for sales Can be open-ended to earn a lot Good for pursuing orders Good for shorter term sales cycle, transactional markets Costs are controlled because commission is only paid on results	Does not encourage loyalty Can drive a short-term approach Sales people might only look to sales revenue, ignoring margin or relationships Some organisations cap earning potential Can lead to over aggressive selling or inappropriate behaviour – seen in some financial markets recently
Commission only As it says – no basic, only earning when selling	Keeps sales costs down Encourages sales people to prospect and push for sales Effective in certain markets Sales people can earn significant incomes	No loyalty from sales people Creates a high level of insecurity due to lack of income Can lead to over pushy sales approaches Can lead to sellers being less than totally honest with prospects

The first two choices are sensible in sectors where you are using a key account or consultative sales approach. They do not put a financial pressure on the seller who is worrying about paying their bills. They can concentrate on the relationships and building the opportunity. The sales management does need to monitor the early stages of the sales process and pay attention to the standards of performance. The bonuses can be structured so parts are payable for completion or achievement of different elements of the job, not just the sales revenue. (I have one client who has part of the bonus tied into using their

CRM system properly.) You can also link bonus systems across other functions, especially sales support or customer service. Many organisations slip up with this approach because they are not willing to have a wide enough band between bottom and top for the newcomers, underperformers through middle of the road to the stars.

The most common is the salary + commission option. The key decisions here are what level to set the salary band at, how this relates to the on-target earnings package, how much commission to offer and what for? Make sure the salary is at a reasonable level so new sellers, or those having a difficult time, are not slipping into financial troubles. (Avoid what a former senior sales manager I knew believed. His view was that if people were struggling to pay their basic bills they would work harder to earn some commission. This was despite the evidence of many leaving for something more secure. In various theories of motivation if people are worried about money and paying for their homes, food, etc., they become demotivated *not* motivated.)

The commission element poses its own questions. When does it start? Once over quota? Over 50% of quota? From the beginning? There is not a perfect answer. Do you put a cap on what someone can earn? (If you do, ask why? What is the incentive to get more business?) How about a sliding scale or accelerator, a higher percentage for more sales? My own view is that if you are using a salary plus commission, keep it open-ended so that your top performers might earn more than their managers. No one should lose because they are only earning this through generating more business for the organisation. The other key question around commission is what you pay it for? Is it only for revenue or sales volume? This might lead to high pressure closing or pushing products. Think about paying it on margin earned or a combination. You can complicate the process with different rates for new business, repeat business or up-selling or additional products. Although you might be able to make a case for this, I would suggest you aim to keep it as simple as possible and related to your sales strategy.

Commission only can work in a few instances, and if using sales agents. However, the downsides with lack of loyalty, insecure sales people feeling under pressure and possible mis-selling outweigh the financial gains in my opinion. In some markets, and some countries, it may be a way forward, but it is not ideal especially if you want to be in any area of relationship or consultative selling.

The other parts of the compensation package matter too. What additional benefits are on offer? Apart from the fairly obvious elements such as holidays, sick pay, insurances and pensions, there will be others. In some markets, what company cars do you have or car schemes? These are often the most emotive part of the package, partly because they are a highly visible statement of someone's level or status. Changes to the policy cause lots of discontent. What other equipment is provided? Smart phones, laptops and tablets are increasingly expected, although a small organisation may not be able to stretch to these. Do you have open-ended allowances for use of phones? What about amounts for hotel stays and entertainment or meals?

Many sales operations like to offer incentives for specific activities or projects, such as weekend breaks, meals out or tickets to a major event for the top performer or the one with the biggest sales growth over the quarter. Some major organisations have trips or 'conferences' for their top achievers. These high-profile rewards work for some people and can provide a reasonably sustained improvement. I do suggest you think about ideas which can be 'won' by more than one person to keep as many as possible engaged. To make these effective, know your people and choose something they will be inspired by whether it appeals to you or not.

There are some other, more intangible options you can introduce. A simple one is using job titles to differentiate levels in the sales operation. I have seen ideas such as ties, tie pins, scarves and brooches used to recognise success or seniority. Giving different cars can also work and a final option is to invite your top performers to a decent venue for a meeting or conference where you involve them in discussing new ways forward, meeting managers from other functions and a bit of relaxation and a good meal. Even in these days of controlling costs, this can be a good investment in providing recognition and making these people feel valued.

The sales manager's checklist

- Do some research about levels of salary in your sector and, if you can, your competition.

- Aim to pitch your package in the top 25% of your market; there should be no need to offer the highest pay – just be competitive and treat people well and fairly.

- Think about which salary option will work best for your sales approach and your market.

- Decide on the specific areas you want to cover with bonuses or commission. Remember, people will do what is inspected and rewarded.

- Make sure the other elements of your overall compensation package are fair within the market.

- Think about identifying some incentive plans or schemes to give the sellers something to aim for.

- Keep checking your reward package and ideas for rewards and incentives and be willing to adapt them to suit changes in the market and to stay fresh.

Establishing your expectations

Objectives

- To understand the importance of clearly communicating the standards and objectives with your sales people
- To identify options for explaining your expectations clearly
- To use these expectations to monitor and maintain performance

Understanding

It is fair to presume that most people, including those in sales, do not intend to underperform or fail to meet their manager's expectations. Which begs the question, why do they? Too often the reason is simple: the expectations are not clear or not expressed succinctly. The managers may talk about them and why they matter. Alternatively, they think that it should be obvious that certain things are expected. There might be some truth in this and maybe the sales people should be mature and sensible in understanding the expectations. Unfortunately, this does not happen very often. If you have a resource costing over £50K a year it might be reasonable for you to have some clear expectations of what you want them to be able to do, and how they will perform; and let them know what these are.

Part five considered 'Setting the direction' and areas around the sales process, standards of performance and monitoring performance. As the manager you need to make sure you have done all of these because they provide the basis for your expectations and what you have to communicate with your sales people. The more rigorous and clear your objectives, sales process definition and standards, the easier it is to explain them to your sales people so that they are clear and unambiguous. This is especially true if you are in a market with a long sales cycle or using a consultative sales approach which might take time.

Most people have a simple list of requirements from their employer:

- Tell me what is expected of me. I want to know what I am supposed to be doing.
- Give me the right skills to do it. If I need training or help, give it to me.
- Give me the resources and support to do the job.
- Tell me how I am doing. (Feedback is a primary motivator for most of us.)
- Recognise and reward success – not necessarily just with money.

If you keep this list in mind it can act as a useful reminder of the importance of making your expectations clear. They provide the basis for better understanding between you all. Another benefit is that it can be a trigger for you to remember to give feedback.

Doing

Establishing expectations of your sales people needs to be addressed in two respects: those for the individual; and those for the sales people as a group. Each of them will probably have their own, specific objectives although there can be some areas which are common to more than one person. The standards of performance should be the same for all, except for possible adjustments for newer sellers. If you are introducing a sales process and implementing a CRM system, technological or manual, these need to be standardised and your expectations applied to all.

The first step towards making your expectations effective is to communicate them clearly. Blend talking with your sales people, individually for their objectives or collectively for standards and the sales process, with confirmation in writing. This might seem over the top to some of you, but the aim is to minimise the risk of misunderstanding from your sales people and reduce any ambiguity. If you have experienced people working for you, it can be more useful to explain what you want and then discuss their thoughts and be open to modifying the detail. Ensure everyone has a copy of all relevant information relating to these expectations. (You can even make some elements of them into posters or similar to promote these and keep them visible and in mind.) As part of this step, let the sales people know why you want to implement these and how the principle should help everyone to be successful.

The second step is to check that everyone understands what you want from them. Allow people to express any concerns they may have or where they anticipate possible problems. Address these and develop or offer some solutions and ways forward. Remember the list from earlier: 'give me the resources and support to do the job'.

The third step is to tell the sellers how you will monitor all of these elements. Agree the regular reviews of progress for the objectives with them individually. The majority of the standards will be monitored through the planning and reporting processes whether in the CRM or separate. Those not covered here will be picked up by observation of day-to-day work.

The fourth step is to do something with this monitoring and checking. Where there is any slippage in the performance, act quickly. Do not allow things to drift so that any correction becomes bigger and more difficult. It is less fraught for all concerned to move when the gap between expectation and delivery is small. When people are doing a good job, making progress towards/ achieving their objectives, exceeding the standards of performance, or using the CRM well, recognise this. Give praise and positive feedback. When your sales people realise you are paying attention to the various expectations they will be more likely to focus on them and want to do well.

The sales manager's checklist

■ Make sure you have identified the objectives for each sales person and that they are SMART.

■ Have a clear understanding of the range of standards of performance you want to use to establish expectations, both qualitative and quantitative.

■ Put everything in writing in order to share with others and to avoid misunderstanding or people forgetting what you expect.

■ Discuss all of these with your sellers when explaining them and to establish understanding and intended actions, whilst allowing any concerns to be raised.

■ Check that your planning and reporting system incorporates ways of monitoring the standards of performance.

■ Pay attention to all of your range of expectations, acting quickly if there is any slip; and acknowledge where there is good performance. Letting people know you are treating these as important means they are more likely to do the same.

Inductions and bringing new people on

Objectives

- To understand the benefits of implementing a structured induction process
- To be able to develop an effective induction programme
- To use the induction programme to assess individual performance

Understanding

Many organisations do not appreciate the value of implementing an effective, structured induction programme for new starters. They may have a cursory set of actions to offer the new people, covering basics such as where their workplace is, paperwork, health and safety, and possibly a few other details. This is high risk for many reasons, not least because the first few days are creating the first impression in the mind of the starter and they will be comparing these with the expectations they have formed from their interviews. Where their impressions are less than favourable, feelings of discontent can form quickly and can lead to people leaving their jobs within the first few weeks or months. Something like 40% of employee turnover occurs within the first three months – an expensive exercise when you look at the initial recruitment costs and have to start all over again. The opposite is true for organisations which have a good induction programme and process. They have a much higher retention rate, develop people to a productive level more quickly – and can identify those who might not make it.

Ideally, the induction process begins before the new person starts. It is also a useful additional item to introduce at the interview so that candidates can see that you take care of new starters. Although you can have a general set of principles and ways to address particular areas, the most effective induction programme blends those with a tailored component to cover specific areas for the individual. With sales people the induction has to cover a wide range, from organisation knowledge, processes and structure, to market and customer awareness, plus the sales process and administration.

The idea of an induction programme is to introduce someone to your organisation, the people, the place and the way everything works and then the fundamentals of their job. (The intricacies will take a bit longer, especially in a sales role.) It does not have to be rushed through in a week. I have set induction programmes for periods of between four and ten weeks in my past when managing people, depending on their roles. Your organisation might need to make them even longer.

Induction training processes and programmes should include the following elements:

- **General topics** relating to the organisation, including values and philosophy as well as structure and history, etc.
- **Mandatory training** covering elements such as health and safety and other essential or legal areas.
- **Job specific training** relating to the role that the new starter will be performing.
- **Evaluation**, checking understanding, development of competence and getting feedback about the training.

The overall process can involve a variety of approaches: formal workshops or training sessions, shadowing colleagues, meetings, handling projects, working on their own, self-study or anything else which works. As already mentioned, the idea is to adapt the detail to suit the individual. It can also add to the strength of the induction to discuss with the individual how they see their own strengths, aims and development needs. This helps to make them feel more valued as an individual.

Doing

If you do not already have one in your organisation, put together an overall induction process incorporating all of the 'general' elements to be covered. Think about drawing up a simple table with the following headings.

- *Topic or item* – Identify the area to address, from organisation background, values and culture through to getting coffee or refreshments, to finding the toilets.
- *Methodology* – How can we do this? Meeting someone, on-line, group workshop, showing them around, observing, shadowing, reading or any other options you have available.
- *Who needs to be involved?* – It is not all on your shoulders (if you have other colleagues). Use the most appropriate person in terms of knowledge of the area being covered combined with personal style when interacting with others.
- *How long?* – Make a judgment about a reasonable length of time to cover the area sufficiently. Please do not expect a new starter to focus for ages on a particular topic; they can always come back and do more later. This is particularly relevant when planning time to be spent meeting people in other functions or shadowing. After a while, the new person might start to feel uncomfortable or as though they are taking the other from their work.
- *Measure?* – How can you evaluate whether the trainee has the right level of understanding or learned the element of the job? Have they achieved it?

When you have an outline for the topics to be covered and an idea of how long might be needed overall, you can think about the most logical sequence to cover them. You can create a general template for use with any new starters. Once you know the person you want to take on you can fill in the more specific areas which will be right for them and enable them to reach a productive level as quickly as possible.

For new sales people you need to include opportunities to learn about your product or service and applications. The sales process, planning and reporting systems have to be understood in addition to how to use any technology available. If you can, allow the newcomer to spend some time out with existing sales people. (If you have some choice, do make sure they go out with those who are working in line with your sales process.) This allows them to develop an understanding of the customers, the marketplace and how to sell what you have on offer.

I think it is a good idea to encourage the newcomer to start to have some time getting on with the job on their own during the overall programme. This might include researching and prospecting or even some days going out on sales calls. There is no substitute for actually doing the job to find out what it really involves.

I know it was a long time ago, but I remember my first week in a full sales job. Day one was spent shadowing an experienced salesman in the morning and at an area sales meeting in the afternoon. Days two and three were shadowing two other colleagues. Day four was out on my own! Something of a shock to my system. It had looked quite easy watching my more experienced colleagues. However, the people I met did not seem to say the right things and it was not quite so easy. Luckily (or was it?) I kept on going and actually got an order on my last call of the day. There was a day with a senior salesman and area manager on the Friday to review how my day went and what we could plan to bring me up to speed and build my knowledge and confidence. Whatever we agreed seemed to work.

Develop the specific induction programme for the individual, mapping out days and weeks, showing activities, location, who is involved, and aims. This can be prepared before the new person starts and given to them either on their first day or even before. It will be helpful for them to see what will be happening, how they will fit in and progress towards being able to do their job. Knowing where they need to be, who they will be meeting and what they will be doing is reassuring. We sometimes forget how uncertain most people are when starting a new job. They arrive with enthusiasm and a positive attitude to their new job and we need to capitalise on this and not allow it to evaporate quickly by allowing doubts and worries to take over.

To make sure the induction process and programme is working, schedule regular reviews with each individual. Look back over the activities covered since your previous meeting, explore what they have learned, what they will do with that, and encourage them to share any aspects they want to revisit or do more on. Look forward to the next week, or longer, and discuss what they will cover, how and what the outcomes are for this stage. Allow the newcomer to raise any concerns or make suggestions about what is planned.

Investing your time in this induction will pay dividends. It will bring people on more quickly, improve staff retention and help you identify anyone who may struggle.

The sales manager's checklist

- Invest time in creating an overall induction process for your organisation, and for the sales operation.

- Create a format or template for the process so that you can use it consistently, and include it as part of your interviewing process.

- Involve colleagues in delivering the induction and make sure they understand the importance of their contribution.

- Develop specific induction programmes for each new starter to address their personal requirements.

- Give the individual their induction programme so that each of you can monitor it.

- Review their progress regularly and be willing to adjust the programme where necessary.

Communicating with your team

Objectives

- To understand the need to communicate effectively with the sales people
- To recognise the need to adapt your communication to suit the individual when appropriate
- To be aware of the advantages and disadvantages of the different communication channels
- To make sales meetings a positive and constructive part of your communication process

Understanding

In these days of technology all around us and with so many different ways of getting and keeping in touch, we have little excuse for not communicating with colleagues, customers and staff. However, does the speed and ease of contacting others really improve communication? I believe that the reality is that we are more concerned with how quickly we can communicate with others rather than how effectively we do it. This can then lead to our communication being ineffective and inefficient because the wrong message can easily be received. None of us intends to miscommunicate but how often do we feel we are misunderstood? If this happens, do not blame the receiver. Take a bit of time and think about what you want to transmit. A phrase I find very helpful is, 'the meaning of my communication is the response I get'. If my message is not getting the response I expect or want, look at myself and what I could have done differently.

Sales people can be a challenge to communicate with, especially if they are working in the field and rarely in the office. They need to be kept informed about a wide variety of things and many want to have someone they can talk to and feel is listening to them. However, some seem to need less interaction and appear more independent. At times they might even appear to resent you calling or messaging them. One of your biggest challenges is to understand the different personalities of those you manage and what they need from you in communication: how often, what methods and what message are all part of the equation.

All of your sales people need to be kept informed about:

- Your expectations of them, individually and collectively.
- How they are performing against these expectations.
- The overall sales progress.
- Things happening in the market – in general, in the customers and for competitors.
- Company information and updates, people, performance and plans.

You also need to communicate with them about how they are doing in general, what their plans look like, and take an interest in them personally.

Many of these interactions will take place directly between you and the individual seller. Some will be more 'collective', either by e-mails or similar to all involved or dealt with at sales meetings. These more collective communication situations need better planning and thinking about. Finding the right tone and emphasis to suit each recipient is important, although not always possible. Sales meetings, in particular, can be a very useful and positive means of communicating with, and involving, your sellers. They can also drift into being boring and demotivating if not handled carefully.

Doing

Think about this topic as one of your key tasks. The quality of your communication with your sales people will be a significant factor in how they view you as a leader. Some participants on a course I was running came up with what I consider to be a really powerful definition of communication: 'To understand and to be understood.' Breaking this down provides food for thought and more effective communication. Start by thinking of the need to understand both the objective of your message and the receivers. These two elements need to happen almost simultaneously because you need to assess the receivers' levels of understanding, likely reactions to your message and their relationship with you. You may adjust your message to accommodate the outcomes of this assessment and improve the chance that you will be understood.

Too often we rush into sending our message without taking a small amount of time to think about these things. The result is misunderstanding or miscommunication, which leads to potential problems. In turn, the message needs to be re-sent and the task or activity done again. Another benefit of keeping the 'to be understood' phrase at the front of your communication process is that it can also help you think about which channel to use, i.e. which method of sending your message.

Channel	Advantages	Disadvantages
Face to face	More personal	Can take more time
	Able to observe body language and response	Can slip into more general chat and lose sight of outcome
	Can encourage discussion	
	Better two-way communication	
Telephone	Time efficient	Can be intrusive
	Fairly immediate	One party might be distracted by other events at their end
	Can pre-plan time to call	
	Good for short messages	No body language
	Relatively easy to do with existing technology	Messages can be misinterpreted

Channel	Advantages	Disadvantages
E-mail	Good for sharing information or giving instructions Can be used for individual or collective communication Able to send additional information Can be readily accessed with modern technology Useful if working across different time zones	Frequently written in haste Messages not always clear and can be misread, causing a negative response Can start e-mail 'chains' Too easy to use rather than speaking directly Too many have an expectation of speed in response or action Care is needed with the cc function
Text message	Short and to the point Immediate Good for simple instructions or responses Good for confirming things Easy to use when out and about	Although 'text speak' has some advantages, not everyone understands it Too easy to slip into a habit, rather than talking to someone
Meetings	Time efficient in sharing messages with a group Can encourage sharing and building on ideas Two-way communication and more	Need planning to pitch message for different people Need managing to keep to agenda and focus on outcomes Some people do not feel comfortable opening up in groups

When considering communicating with your sales people, think about the message, the desired outcome and the individual character. Only then, decide on the content and structure of your message and the best channel to use. This might change because some of your people are comfortable with the telephone and short interactions; others prefer face-to-face meeting and longer discussions. Be flexible and adapt your approach to improve the effectiveness of your communication.

Although you might have some informal group meetings, it is probable that you want to introduce more structured and regular sales meetings. How can you do this, without triggering a collective groan? Make them feel it is worth their time being at the meeting. There is no guaranteed formula for success, but there are some guidelines which might help. In principle there is no real difference between most of these points and any other successful meeting. Do remember that all meetings are costly when you calculate the amount of time spent in total man hours and multiply it by each person's hourly on-cost to the organisation. (I said in Part four when looking at the costs of the sales function, that your sales people cost about £50 per hour. By the time they travel to the meeting, attend it and then travel back they have incurred a substantial charge. You also have to add on your time and any other people attending from other functions.)

I suggest starting with a simple checklist:

1 What is the main outcome for the meeting?
2 What other outcomes do I have from the meeting?
3 [*List them ...*]
4 What other ways could I use to achieve these outcomes?
5 Which will I use?

Technology does give you some other options for meetings. Do you always need to physically get together or can you do some using video conferencing? I do not advocate that all meetings are held this way, but having a blend of on-line and physical is the way forward.

- When you have decided that you will have a sales meeting, there are some other things to think about.
- Where are you going to hold the meeting? (Consider where people have to travel from. It can be good to move the

meeting around if budgets allow, so as to provide some variety of venue.)

- When are you going to have the meeting? (Best time of day?)
- How long do we need? Set a start and finish time – and stick to them. (Do not wait for the last person to drift in.)
- Who should attend? (Is it useful to invite some people from other functions to contribute or learn about yours?)
- Who, from all the attendees, can you use to present some part of the meeting? (Change of face and voice can be good, provided there is a purpose. It is not all on your shoulders.)
- When do we need the next meeting?
- Create an agenda – and think about options. Do not spend too long just analysing figures.
- Circulate the agenda to all attendees beforehand and ask for any other topics for inclusion. Allow them if you have time and avoid AOB (any other business).
- Within the framework of the meeting, focus on and share successes to learn from them. Allow time to develop new ideas.

ALWAYS aim to have people leaving the meeting feeling as though it was worth attending.

The sales manager's checklist

- Keep the need to communicate with your sales people high on your priority list.
- Be aware of your own preferred style and methods of communication and how these influence your own approach.
- Understand your sales people and think about their communication preference. Use this when interacting with them. It will improve effectiveness.

■ Remember, communicating with your people should be about more than just giving information or instructions.

■ Plan your message and method of communication.

■ Use the checklist and planning list for your sales meetings so that they are worthwhile for all involved.

Managing and growing performance

The need for leadership

Objectives

- To recognise the fundamental differences between management and leadership
- To understand the importance of providing leadership for your sales people
- To understand the need to adapt your leadership approach to suit the individual

Understanding

In Parts four to six the focus has been on the management elements of running the sales operation. These are very necessary, just as in any other area of the organisation. However, to maximise the probability of achieving the desired results you also need to provide effective leadership. The majority of people like to have a leader helping to provide the direction that they are expected to go in and the support to do so.

Management 'Doing things right'	Leadership 'Doing the right things'
Management is about getting things done.	Leadership is the development of a vision and direction.
It requires co-ordination of resources to achieve a defined end result (objective or target).	It is about inspiring, involving, developing people and keeping them motivated.
Management is about processes and tasks.	Leadership is mostly about behaviour and people.

Management and leadership are not mutually exclusive. You can be a strong manager offering little leadership and it is possible to achieve results, although it will be harder work because the people may not be engaged or motivated. You can be a good leader without many management skills or qualities. This is also likely to be less than fully effective, especially in difficult times because the control and monitoring may not happen. Bringing the two together is your best way forward.

Leadership is a word that can cause a great deal of debate. If you ask a group of people to define it, you will probably get different definitions from each person. Within your own organisation, you might have one interpretation from your boss, another from those who report to you and further ideas from your peers. Who is right? Everyone and no one. Although we can talk around what the leader does, as shown in the table, how it is perceived will vary. This is even more pronounced when you start to look at leadership styles and try to define yours. Regardless of your opinion, what you think it might be does not matter. The people who decide on your style are those you are leading. This means each might have their own idea of your leadership style, despite you doing your best to behave consistently and fairly.

When looking at leadership, there are three levels: task, operational and strategic. Although there are some similarities in the qualities and requirements across all three levels, there are differences too. Senior managers and leaders need to provide the medium- and long-term vision. Their leadership style and

approach needs to keep people focused on that horizon and make sure that the organisation is set up to work towards it. (This relates to the areas covered in Part four.) The other leaders, whether in middle or first line management, are more functional. They need to provide the vision, direction and plan to achieve more specific tasks or activities in a shorter or even immediate timescale. When leading and managing a sales operation and sales people you might find you need to be able to move between all three levels.

Doing

Some people appear to be natural leaders and take on the role in many situations, both in and out of the workplace. Whilst this can be good much of the time, it does not mean they will be effective sales leaders in all situations. Their style and approach might not fit. If you do not feel you are in the natural leader category, do not worry – you can still develop your leadership skills and potential.

It is important to recognise that effective leadership is an ongoing challenge. The demands of the different personalities you have to lead combined with those of the situations which occur provide a wide spectrum. You need to be able to adapt to suit the specific needs at the time. Whatever you do will be viewed by those you are leading and they will each apply their own, unique perspective of you and your leadership style. Some might think it exactly right and others could consider you as too controlling or too laid back. It is very tricky to get it right for most of the people most of the time.

When thinking about your own leadership, check how well you measure up with the qualities listed below:

- *Integrity* – being open and truthful (as far as you can) in order to generate trust.
- *Positive* – a belief in what is possible, focusing on what can be achieved, projecting the right level of enthusiasm without going over the top.

- *Determined* – willing to persevere through challenges, to overcome setbacks.

- *Sincere* – linked with integrity, being true and not creating false hope or making rash promises.

- *Sensitive* – having an awareness of sales people, what is happening for them, when to offer support, when to push.

- *Toughness* – setting and following through on high standards, expecting people to perform, at the same time being consistent and fair, making decisions.

- *Humility* – open to learning, asking for others' ideas and input (colleagues and sales people), giving credit to others.

- *Warmth* – interested in others, being approachable.

- *Communication* – sharing information, providing the vision, listening, listening, listening.

- *Developer* – bringing out the best in others, delegating, coaching, training.

Although there are many leadership models which you can use, I believe that 'Situational Leadership' can be the most useful for you. It starts with a fundamental principle about the balance between the leader's concern for results or achieving goals and their concern for the people or relationship. As you can see from the diagram below, this gives the leader a choice of four fundamental styles they can use. When you look at these options there is one which looks as though it would be most people's preference: the high task, high relationship quadrant. (The task axis is talking about the amount of direction and instruction the leader gives about what the task is, how it needs to be done, timescales etc. The relationship axis is looking at the personal interaction and how much dialogue is involved. It is *not* about how approachable the leader is or whether they like the person.) There are two quadrants which you might be comfortable with some of the time, but who would want to admit to being in the low task, low relationship area?

STYLE OF LEADER

	LOW TASK HIGH RELATIONSHIP	HIGH TASK HIGH RELATIONSHIP
	LOW TASK LOW RELATIONSHIP	HIGH TASK LOW RELATIONSHIP

High

Relationship behaviour

Low

Low   High

Task or goal behaviour

Where Situational Leadership is different from most approaches to leadership is that it puts the focus onto the 'followers' rather than the leader. Rather than worrying about the leader and their style, shouldn't the focus be put on to the followers and what would work best for them? If you have five people to lead, why would one style be right for all of them all of the time? You are dealing with five different personalities, who probably have different skill or capability levels for each of their key tasks, and also bring different attitudes to these tasks. This is especially true within sales operations and the range of activities that need to be addressed. With all of those variables, one leadership style is only likely to hit the spot some of the time. The skilful leader recognises they need to be flexible to adapt to suit the individual and the situation.

The work originally done by Hersey and Blanchard when working at UCLA suggested looking at the 'followers' and assessing them before deciding on the most effective style to use. They talked about the followers' 'maturity' level. This can be considered in two areas: their 'task maturity', which refers to the skill and capability level for the specific task, and their 'willingness maturity', which is their attitude and approach to the task. A key element to consider when looking at Situational Leadership and the follower is that it is task specific. There are some areas of our work which we are skilled at and enjoy doing; others where we struggle with the task but are enthusiastic and want to do it better; those where we have the skills but dislike doing it and have to be pushed into it. All combinations are possible!

The maturity levels were broken down into four groups.

M1 – People at this level lack the knowledge, skills, or confidence to work on their own, and they often need to be pushed to take the task on.

M2 – At this level, followers might be willing to work on the task, but they still don't have the skills to do it successfully without some support or guidance.

M3 – Here, followers are ready and willing to help with the task. They have demonstrated their capability with the task, but they still might not be fully confident in their abilities.

M4 – These followers are able to work on their own and have shown this and enjoy some degree of independence. They have high confidence and strong skills, and they're committed to the task.

How do you adapt your style to be more effective? The figure below shows you how to aim for the best fit. You can see how the maturity scale for the followers runs across. You work out where the follower is for the specific task and look straight up and see where you meet the curve.

For someone at M1, use the S1 style – telling or directing. You give the clear instructions and guidelines, with very little two-way communication or questions.

Moving to M2, use S2 – selling or coaching. You are still giving the guidance and setting the direction. This time there is more discussion and interaction, questions and explanation. This is a natural style for many leaders. However, it has its limitations with the new starter, the underperformer or, at the other end, with those who are competent and delivering good results.

M3 requires you to use S3 – participating or joining. This step is

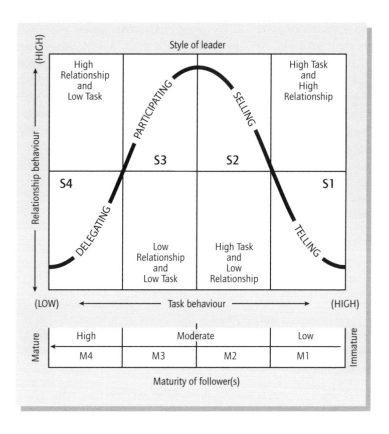

often a challenge for many leaders. The biggest shift here is that you are doing less directing and letting go of some of the control. You want more input and ideas from the follower and are open to considering their suggestions. Consider using it with those who are delivering results consistently and are ready to operate with more freedom.

M4 goes to S4 – delegating. Allowing the follower even more freedom to get on with the task, with little discussion about the detail or the way they will do it. The leader will still monitor without interfering. Your experienced and successful sales people will enjoy this and you need to hold back from delivering too much guidance and direction.

Although you will have a preferred 'natural' style, probably with another back-up one, to be a really effective leader you need to develop the flexibility to move across all four of the styles. The key to effective leadership is to find the right style for each follower and the task – adapting to the situation.

The sales leader's checklist

- Take time to recognise the difference between management and leadership. Identify which of your tasks and activities fit under the leadership category.

- Be careful not to 'over-manage and under-lead'.

- Remember when to move between the three levels of leadership.

- Assess yourself against the leadership qualities and identify areas for improvement. What will you do about these?

- Think about each of your sales people and identify where they are on the M1–M4 scale for both task and willingness for each of their key result areas or job functions.

- Adapt your style to fit with your assessment. If it does not seem to be working, move to another style.

- Keep on top of this because people move between the M levels.

- Be kind to yourself – leadership is an imprecise science!

Coaching to develop performance

Objectives

- To understand the importance of actually observing your sales people making calls
- To know how to act when carrying out the observations in order to not take over the call
- To be able to use a structured approach to reviewing the call
- To be able to use a simple coaching process with your sales people

Understanding

As the previous chapter stressed, seeing yourself as a developer is a key element of your leadership role. If you neglect this, there is a probability that your resources (i.e. people) will not become more productive. In fact, the risk is that their performance will gradually slip. Even if they stay at the same level of competency, their performance might erode because markets, customers and your own organisation are moving forward, which leaves them behind. When you want to grow performance and aim to develop your people, you need to assess how they are doing. What is going well? What could be better?

I am fascinated by the number of Sales Managers, or those responsible for sales in their organisations, who talk about developing their people and might send them on sales training courses. However, when pressed, their view of how well their sales people are doing is frequently only based on the actual results being achieved, occasionally combined with looking at some of their reports or information put into the CRM or record system. To me, that is like a top tennis coach saying that they only need to look at their player's results and maybe some reports on their matches in order to develop their people. How can you identify how your sales people are really performing, their strengths and areas for development if you do not witness them first hand?

I was shocked during a training programme I was delivering recently. One of the participants told me that her sales manager (who only had a team of three) had never been out with her for a day in the field in the six months she had been with the company. Apart from being staggered by this, and why he was able to get away with not supporting his sales people, I did wonder what he actually did with his time. I was also intrigued by how he would conduct the performance reviews.

As covered earlier, the sales results come from the right activity into the right potential. You can use your CRM or other reporting systems to monitor these. However, these do not tell what happens during the call. Are they following your sales process? What exactly are they doing? This is particularly relevant if they appear to have the right activity levels and are meeting enough potential people but are missing the results you need. Unless you are there to witness what is happening, you cannot offer help and support. (Please, do not do what I see too many sales managers doing: applying pressure on the struggling sales person is unlikely to raise their performance, without specific focus or guidelines. That just builds your stress level and theirs.)

Be honest with yourself about why you are not doing the observations. You may be really busy and under time pressure. Who is not, these days? I believe you will probably add to your time pressure by trying to lead and develop your sales people from behind a desk. Is the real reason that you do not know how you should act if observing? What is your role during the calls?

A number of benefits will be gained from spending time observing your sales people. A significant one is that you can get to know them better. You can find out more about them as a person, their interests, aims, ambitions, concerns or worries. By observing them during actual calls you can compare what they are doing with the sales process and competencies needed. In addition to identifying any area for development, you get the opportunity to give positive feedback too. I will explain how to set up the day, and manage the call so that it will be good for all concerned. You will then be in a good position to offer constructive support and coach your sales people. This is not some mystical art: more a simple and clear process.

Doing

When organising your observation visits (the principles will also apply if you are spending time with inside sales people, although you are unlikely to spend all day with an individual), make sure you schedule them in advance in your time planner. My view is that you should be aiming to plan to spend about a day a month with each sales person. With new starters this might be more frequent and for some experienced sellers it might be a bit less. One of the key tasks you have in adopting this approach is to create a sales culture where these observation, or dual calling, days are considered to be the way you do things. The sales people need to accept this and if they feel threatened or concerned – tough. After all, you need to see how your £52K resource is doing.

Suggestions for your dual calling day

Arranging the day

- Plan ahead and explain the purpose to the sales person.
- It is important to arrange a 'typical' day.
- Make sure you plan to spend the day with them (very occasionally a part day might be acceptable).

When and where to meet

- Meet them either on their territory or close to it and early.
- They need to be able to make the first visit at the start of the day and not mid-morning.
- Choose a meeting time and place where you can talk about the day ahead and any other issues in a relaxed way.
- Be early or on time. (You have to be the role model.)
- Do not finish early.

Agree the aims and process for the day

- Discuss the planned visits and overall aim of the day.
- Agree how you will be introduced and how you will act during the visits.
- Explain what you want to get from the day and how and when you will give any feedback.
- If there are specific aspects of their sales skills you want to look at, share this.

The sales call itself

- Talk over the history of the account, objectives for the call, any specific issues and possible objections.
- Keep a low profile, position yourself slightly to one side if you can. If the prospect tries to move the conversation to you, turn it back to the seller using verbal and non-verbal messages.
- If you feel you have to step in or redirect the call, do it with questions not statements.
- Avoid making special concessions to get the order – it is a dangerous precedent with the account *and* it undermines your seller.

After the call ('The kerbside conference')

- You do not need to do a full review after each call.
- A brief recap of how it went and tie this to the call objectives.
- Have the sales person start and encourage them to do most of the talking.
- Focus on what is done well.
- If you need to highlight an area for attention, do so in a constructive way, but do not labour it.

Summarise the day

- Choose somewhere to sit and spend time to review the day in a relaxed manner.

- Ask for their impressions of the day and then specific calls.
- What went well? What can be improved?
- Give your thoughts, emphasising where they have improved (if relevant).
- Identify two or three key areas to improve at the most.
- Use the 'ROAR' coaching process (see below).
- Leave them on a positive note – and set the next dual calling day.

Remember, your effectiveness will be shown by what the sales person does after the visit. I would recommend you make your own notes to summarise what you observed, what was agreed in the 'ROAR' process and how you will support this and follow-up.

The coaching part of the job is not as difficult as many managers imagine. You do not have to be the expert, nor an instructor. *Coaching is* **not** *instructing or training another.* Coaching is working with others to encourage them to grow and develop. It involves support and challenge of others to help them move forward. It can be defined as *the art of facilitating the performance, learning and development of another* and is about using day-to-day events and work as learning experiences.

There are many ideas and models about coaching. The core elements for you to consider are: identifying the specific performance gap between what you observed and what you need to see as the actual level; getting agreement about this gap; listening carefully and using good questioning skills. If you approach coaching with the right intentions and encourage the other person to speak and develop their own ideas, with the right probing, balancing support and challenge you will do a good job.

Working with sales people, the 'ROAR' process can be highly effective. It is easy to remember and can be quick to work through when an area is identified for development.

The questions shown below are only indicators and you do not have to use all of them in each step!

R – RIGHT NOW (What is happening? What did you observe?)

- What has to be done to …? And why?
- What do think of the way you …?
- What could you do differently/better?
- What would you like to be able to achieve?
- What do you think is the reason for …?
- What does your instinct say you could do?
- What result did you get when you …? Was that what you wanted?
- What are the challenges you have with doing …? What problems that gives you?

O – OPTIONS (What options or idea do you have for improving or correcting the situation?)

- What else could you do?
- What other ways do you think you could …?
- How else could you …?
- What ideas do have for …?
- What other things do you need to consider?
- Which option do you think would give you the best results?
- Do you want me to suggest some options?
- What would you see as the advantages and disadvantages with each option?
- On a scale of 1–10, how attractive is each option?

A – ACTION (Agreeing on the specific actions the individual will take – and creating an action plan)

- What steps do you need to take?
- What will you do first?
- What might stop you …? What can you do about it?

Now step back and observe. Compare the behaviour and outcomes with what was discussed and agreed. (And give time and space for the person to complete the task.)

R – REVIEW – at an agreed future date (considering how things went, what they achieved and learned and agreeing the next steps)

- How do you feel that went?
- What went well? Why do you think that was?
- What could have gone better? Why do you think that was?
- What will you do differently next time?
- What have you learned from this?
- What could prevent you being successful next time? How will you overcome this?
- What other support or help do you need from me, or others?

You will find that it becomes easier to use this as you become more familiar with the flow and your confidence grows. Another 'micro-coaching' approach is to use these questions:

- 'How do you think that went?'
- 'What do you feel you did well?'
- 'What would you do differently if you could do it again?' or 'What will you do differently in the future?'

The sales leader's checklist

- Make observing your sales people one of your high priority tasks.
- Schedule regular observation visits with your sales people.
- Set the days up properly, using the guidelines shown.
- Remember, a large part of your success as a coach will be due to you adopting a positive attitude to it.
- Be kind to yourself: you will get better with time and practice.
- Develop your questions within the 'ROAR' process so that you use ones which are comfortable for you.

- Create the culture where dual calling and ongoing coaching become part of the way you do things and everyone feels more comfortable with it.

Motivating your team

Objectives

- To understand the range of factors which motivate people
- To recognise how to reduce the risk, and impact, of demotivators on your sales people
- To understand the importance of knowing your people and their individual motivation drivers

Understanding

Let me start by challenging the myth that all sales people are motivated by money, and chase an ever-rising commission or bonus. This may apply to a tiny minority and they will choose organisations, and sales sectors, which will reward them accordingly. However, there are many different types of people in sales and they have a wide range of motivational drivers apart from money. Yes, they want to be fairly rewarded for what they do, but money is only part of that equation. They are not a different species to others in the workforce.

What is motivation? The root of the word is Medieval Latin, *'Motivus'* – 'serving to move'. Motivation is when we feel we want to, or need to, behave in a certain way and sustain it. It is a driving force. However, what motivates any of us changes throughout our lives, and potentially on a daily basis. A wide range of factors can change what motivates us. Add to that, no two people are exactly the same in the way they respond to events: one person's motivator can be another's demotivator and yet another could be indifferent to them. To get the best from your sales people (and yourself), it is important to have some understanding of the principles of motivation to keep them engaged and committed.

A lot has been written about motivation, with various concepts being proposed. In my experience, there is not one 'right' model, nor is one better than another. Although they have their own background and ideas, they can all be useful to help you build your understanding. In turn, the awareness can give you more ideas and options for dealing with your people.

The concepts have tended to evolve as our understanding of people and psychology has increased. Another factor influencing motivation is the rapid pace of change and the impact on organisations. Alongside this is what is happening on a wider basis, with the Generation Y or Millennial Generation group forming more of the workforce, bringing their expectations, closely followed by the latest group, Generation Z. They want things to happen more quickly, expecting to be given more opportunities for growth or promotion in shorter timescales, and having less perseverance with tasks. These views may be true for some of the younger people, but they are unfair generalisations for many. Even the way they gather information, communicate and expect to be communicated with is different and needs to be understood.

It is not essential for you to know lots of theories of motivation, nor do you only have to focus on the newest ones. In fact, two of the older, and most established, still have much to offer. Abraham Maslow is associated with the 'needs' approach to motivation. The various needs are shown in the figure below. It is referred to as a hierarchy, not because it is 'better' to have your needs at a higher level, but rather that there is an ascending order where the lower level has to be reasonably satisfied before the next one comes into focus. For example, if the basic and physiology level is not satisfied because you cannot afford to buy food or pay for heating, you are not too bothered about how you get on with your team colleagues (belonging), or achieving the latest objectives you have been given (ego and esteem).

The core components of each need level are:

- *Basic and physiological:* air, food, water, heat, shelter, sleep
- *Safety and security:* job security, health, family, stability, protection (insurance, etc.)
- *Belonging*: family, affection, acceptance, friendships, team colleagues, social groups

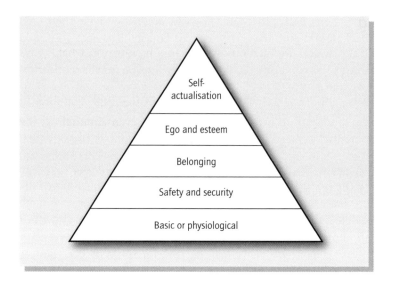

- *Ego and esteem*: achievement, self-esteem, recognition of others, status

- *Self-actualisation*: feeling of fulfilling potential, stimulation, personal growth, creativity, freedom of thinking.

If the need is satisfied, it is not a significant driver. However, if the need is too high it can be a demotivator. Rumours of redundancy will not make people more motivated to perform – their security need becomes undermined. This becomes the individual's primary focus and concern.

How well do you know your people? Where do you think they are on each level? Where do they want to be?

There are other ideas put forward, such as Herzberg's two-factor theory which lists elements providing long-term satisfaction and those which can be significant dissatisfiers. His work, subsequently built upon by a number of others, is that the most powerful and lasting contributors for motivation are primarily intrinsic. We make our own choice to respond to these positively. Our managers or leaders cannot make us feel motivated by these.

Doing

If the most powerful motivation factors are intrinsic, what is your role as the manager? How responsible are you for the motivation of your people? My view is that you need to provide the right climate for the motivators to flourish. To help this, you need to pay attention to working on reducing, or even eliminating, the potential demotivators. These tend to be more extrinsic, which means you can have more influence over them. There are other factors tied in with people's personality profile and preferred styles, but we do not have space to go into those here.

Some of the typical areas providing demotivation, as identified by Herzberg, are:

- *Company policy* – systems, administration, rules and other similar factors.
- *Supervision* – style of management, degree of monitoring, inconsistency, lack of fairness.
- *Relationship with boss* – How approachable are they? Do you get on with them?
- *Work conditions* – physical environment, working hours, changes to these.
- *Salary* – Is it fair for what I am expected to do? Is it competitive for my job?
- *Relationship with peers* – How well do I get on with the others?
- *Security* – Is my job secure? Is there a threat to it or me?

You may not have a direct input to these. However, it is possible for you to reduce the negative impact through your communication around these areas. Aim to prevent people moaning about these and keep attention on the positive, intrinsic factors. This is particularly important with field-based sales people. Spending time on their own, driving or working from home, provides too much opportunity for thinking and worrying! Despite the need for sellers to have a positive attitude, many have imaginations which lead the other way.

When thinking about intrinsic motivation, Daniel Pink identified three elements, which are easy to remember, although not always easy to apply.

Autonomy

Giving people a degree of freedom about what they do, how and when. Keeping within the organisation rules, think about how you can give freedom and flexibility. It can pay dividends if you can be less directive and more empowering.

Mastery

If we are involved with our work and enjoy it we will want to develop and stretch ourselves.

It starts with the 'mind set' where we believe we can continue to improve, the 'stretch' which needs effort and practice, and it is 'progressive' because you can always do something better.

Purpose

Most of us have a sense of purpose and want to feel we are working towards it. The clearer our sense of purpose, almost like our personal vision, the more we can direct our energies into activities which lead towards it.

Too many organisations do not appreciate the power of these three elements. The managers think their role is focusing on extrinsic factors to motivate their people. These will only produce a short-term effect and need to be repeated again and again. Understand the power of the intrinsic elements and allow them room to blossom. The results will follow.

More power is produced when a person wants something they themselves have decided to go for.

The sales leader's checklist

- Get to know each of your people to understand what drives them. Be aware of any changes in their circumstances which will impact on this.

- Remember, money is not the main motivator for the majority of sales people.

- Each person is motivated by different things. There is not a 'one size fits all' for your sales people.

- The most powerful, medium- and long-term motivators are intrinsic. The individual decides what works for them and how much.

- Another good choice is to provide positive, constructive feedback – and praise.

- Understand the demotivational factors and work hard to minimise or eliminate them for your people.

- Motivation is not your responsibility. Avoiding demotivation is.

- Work hard to create the environment for motivation to flourish.

Reviewing sales performance

Objectives

- To understand the importance of carrying out regular reviews with your sales people
- To know how to make the reviews constructive and developmental
- To recognise the importance of giving clear feedback
- To use the reviews to set the way forward for even better performance

Understanding

Many organisations have some form of appraisal or performance development review system in place. In principle this seems like a good thing; in practice they are often of limited value. A major reason is that they are usually an annual event. This leads to various issues such as: a lack of preparation by both sides; no follow through with plans or promises; reviewing of goals which are irrelevant due to changes in markets or the organisation over the year. These are only a few. It intrigues me why more managers do not carry out regular reviews and find all sorts of excuses for not doing them.

In Part six, when looking at establishing the expectations of the sales people I suggested that we all have an informal 'contract' with our organisations where we want to know what is expected of us and to be told how we are doing. We all like to know whether our work is good or otherwise and sometimes it is nice to be told. As a manager you can think of regular reviews as a way of reinforcing your control of the sales process and keeping things on track. Rather than just relying on what you see in your planning or reporting system, it is more informative and valuable to talk to your sales people.

Creating a habit of having regular reviews has benefits, in many ways, for you, the organisation and the sales people. Some of these include:

- Improved communication between you (and hopefully a better relationship)
- Ability to correct any issues or potential problems early
- Opportunity for sales people to share any concerns or issues
- Opportunity to explore ambitions or potential
- You have to give feedback on how they are doing
- Chance to discuss specific accounts
- Review ongoing performance and set goals for next period of time
- Introduce any changes to adapt to market conditions.

The regular reviews can be varied in frequency and formality. They will also help if you do have any type of annual system because it makes the planning and preparation easy as you are just consolidating the ongoing reviews and, hopefully, the communication between you and your sales people flows smoothly. The exact timing is something you can decide upon, accounting for both your organisation's needs and the sales person. Some might benefit from more frequent meeting and review because of their own personality, others need less (although remember you need to have some reviews from your perspective), and when anyone is struggling you need to be reviewing things with them.

Bearing in mind that these sales people are your main resource and they deliver the results you have to achieve, is it unreasonable to make time to carry out regular reviews for the reasons listed above? Are you avoiding doing them, claiming you are too busy with other activities? For me, these reviews, like dual call days, should be in your highest priority category. Be honest with yourself: do you avoid them because you feel uncomfortable doing them and having to give feedback? Maybe there is a good reason, that you are not sure how to do them?

Doing

You need to have some data to use to assess what your people are doing and how well from your monitoring and control systems. It will be more useful if you have started making field visits to see how your people are when with prospects and customers. The key for any review is to have a baseline of information to review against. I am presuming you know what you would expect from your sales people and the information lets you know whether you are reviewing a successful seller or a struggling one. Either way, the principles will be the same.

To make regular reviews effective for all concerned, you need to get the right blend between a formal meeting and informality. You want all to take it seriously whilst being relaxed and seeing it as a positive time. Begin by explaining to your sales people why you want to introduce the process and what you want to achieve for all of you. Give an overview of how you want the reviews to work and what you would expect from the sales people in terms of preparation and their approach.

I suggest you use something like the steps below to implement ongoing reviews:

1 Always give the sales people notice of when you want to meet for the review, subject to both diaries agreeing a time. The meetings do not always have to be at your office. Fit in with other logistical factors about location for you both. However, always choose somewhere private or quiet where you can have a proper conversation with no interruptions or distractions. This time must be fixed and not moved by either of you.

2 Explain any specific areas you want to be prepared and what you want to achieve from it.

3   When you meet, the following flow can be very effective:

Stage	Process	Person
Past	What can be improved?	Their views
		Your views
	What went well?	Their views
		Your views
	Agree and summarise	Both
Future – plans and actions	Their suggestions	Them
	Your suggestions	You
	Agree and summarise	Both
Help and support	What do they need?	Them
	What do you think?	You
	Where can it come from?	Both
	Agreed actions	

4   Record any agreed actions and follow-up to confirm them.

5   Make a diary note to provide any follow-up or check – and for the next review.

6   Leave them feeling it has been a positive experience.

I have not suggested a time for these, because you might need to be flexible. As a general guide I would say that you should aim to allow about an hour, although this can move either way depending on what you need to cover and the individual you are meeting. However, do not leave it open-ended. This carries the risk of things just drifting on.

A key element of an effective review, and your coaching interactions, is being able to give constructive feedback. This word can give shivers to many managers. They recognise that they need to give it but are neither comfortable nor good at giving it. There are some good reasons for this. Typically, they may not have had many good role models to copy. Additionally, they will have had no guidance or training in how to do it.

What is feedback?

Feedback: Any communication, verbal or non-verbal, which offers a person some information about how their behaviour or actions affect others.

I do not differentiate between 'positive' or 'negative' feedback. As the definition above says, the feedback might be about either positive or negative *behaviour.*

When you are going to give feedback:

- Make sure that you are feeling calm and clear about what you are going to give feedback on.
- Make sure the person you are giving feedback to is open to receiving it. This is a process between consenting adults, not a battle.
- Be specific, quote examples, say what you saw or heard, use evidence to state what you thought the result was. Avoid generalised statements.
- 'Own' the feedback. Use 'I ...' not 'Others told me ...' or 'People have been saying ...'
- Give at least as much 'positive' feedback as 'could have done better'.
- Don't criticise people for what they cannot help: talk about behaviour, not personality.
- Be timely. Don't wait for a month, or for the annual appraisal – it's too late by then.
- Make sure that the environment is right. If giving feedback on any element of underperformance or negative behaviour, it *must* be done in private.
- Do not overload with feedback, watch for the signs. A little and often has more value.

Key points to remember:

1   Focus on what you see – *not on what you believe*
2   Focus on behaviour – *not on personality*
3   It is for their benefit – *not for you to feel better*

4 Use it to inform – *not to advise*

5 Make it supportive – *rather than threatening*

6 Keep it simple – *don't overdo it.*

The sales leader's checklist

▓ Decide that carrying out regular reviews will be one of your high priority activities.

▓ Make time to gather information and prepare for reviews. Use field visits to add to your understanding of the individual.

▓ Think about the review as a combination of your monitoring process and a development opportunity for the sales person.

▓ Aim to make the review a constructive meeting, not just a criticism session.

▓ If things are not going well for the sales person, this is a good opportunity to find out why.

▓ Practise giving feedback in small amounts until you become more comfortable with it.

▓ Find the right balance for frequency and detail level of reviews to make them valuable for you and the individual. It is OK to be flexible in your approach to them.

▓ Recognise that it will take time to generate the positive culture for the reviews to become an embedded part of the way the sales function works. It will be a worthwhile investment.

Dealing with underperformers

Objectives

- To be able to identify which route to take with underperformers
- To understand how to create, and implement, a corrective plan where appropriate
- To be able to give a clear warning to those who are unwilling to change.

Understanding

Managing people, in any function, who are doing a reasonable, or even a good, job is relatively easy. The challenge for many managers is handling those who are underperforming. There are many reasons for this. The majority of us want a peaceful life and prefer to avoid conflicts, disagreements and similar situations. However, there comes a time when you have to confront the issue. Sales people who are underperforming are costly in a number of ways. They cost your company about the same as a productive sales person in direct costs (but without delivering the return on investment). The other areas of cost include lost revenue from their territories, possible loss of relationships or reputation with customers, and additional workload on others having to cover for them.

Too many managers tend to look the other way when they have someone not hitting targets and hope that things will change. Some may make direct or indirect comments which they think might trigger a change, but this is not explicit enough and does not help anyone. No one said management was an easy ride. You need to make effective use of *all* of your resources. If some are not delivering, you are unlikely to achieve your objectives.

Part five emphasised the need to have the right sales process and the controls. You need to be able to monitor the activity levels and to be aware of whether the sales people are contacting the right potential prospects. If a sales person is underperforming, you should have had some early warning that this was probable. Rather than wait for the actual sales results to be below target, step in earlier. If your sales lead time is three months, identifying the problem when you see results are below what is needed will take several months to come through and that is presuming the corrective actions are working.

The reality is that you need to be willing to act quickly. If one of your sales people is not meeting your standards of performance in the activity levels, address the issue. Showing that you take these seriously is a good message to send out. It is usually easier to make the change in the early steps of the process rather than when someone is failing to deliver sales. There tends to be less stress for all concerned.

Before deciding on how you will deal with any underperformers, it is important to identify one critical factor. Ask a simple question: 'Is this because they can't do it or they won't do it?'

The answer leads you down one of two very different routes. If the response is that they won't do it, there is an attitude problem. The 'can't do' option is more skills related and requires some different options. Whichever it is, you must take action. You cannot afford to have underperforming sales people. Not only do they limit your chances of achieving your objectives, they can also have an effect on the morale of the others around them and it does not do much for your credibility if you appear to be tolerating them. The consequence of doing nothing will lead to an even bigger challenge – eventually, you will have to dismiss them.

One point to recognise is that if a sales person is relatively new and underperforming, you might need to accept that you made a mistake in recruiting them. Why else are they not able to do what you require?

Doing

Handling underperforming sales people is not something you can avoid. When you have established the reason for the situation you can decide on which route to take.

The first step to take, once you have recognised that there is a performance issue, is to talk to the individual. You need to have gathered your information so that you can handle this in an objective way. Be quite specific about why you have arranged the meeting and your concerns. Ask the sales person for their views on the situation and their ideas of the reasons for it. (Allow them to talk it through, without interrupting them, even if you do not agree.) Explain what you require or expect and ask how they feel about this. You can be direct and challenge them about whether they are willing or able to do this. The response will dictate your next actions.

Can't do: This suggests that the person needs some additional skills or confidence. You need to work with them to identify the specific areas for development. Agree what you can do to help them and how. Set out a plan to achieve this, using whatever options will work: coaching, shadowing, training courses, are some. Set a timescale which is appropriate for your sales sector and approach, putting in checkpoints to review progress. Give regular feedback and encouragement. If someone wants to make it, give them opportunity to do so.

However, even with all of the coaching and development work, there is still the possibility that some people will not be able to perform. There might be some good reasons for this, one of which is that they are just not right for the role as it stands. Rather than dragging things out, which is not good for anyone, you need to act. Is there an option to move them to another role in your organisation which might suit their skills? If not, then you will have to remove them, following the proper process.

Won't do: This can be more challenging for many managers. You are dealing with an attitude problem, and the only person who can change this is the individual concerned. I believe the best way to tackle this is to be direct. You can have a conversation about why they are unwilling to do what is required and you may take their views into consideration. At the end of the day, you have identified and set the standards you expect and they are not for negotiation with each individual, especially underperformers.

Reiterate why you need these standards to be met. State what has to be done and the consequences if the sales person does not meet them. There might be an underlying issue with their skills and confidence which they are masking with their unwilling attitude. However, this has to change first if they are going to be open to addressing the skills gap. They have to realise that they cannot carry on with their attitude as it is.

This is more effective if you keep calm and state what you expect clearly. Use phrases such as 'I want you to …', or 'I expect you to …' and not 'It would be better if …', or 'I would like you to …'. You can set a correction plan in place, with short-term activity targets relating to the key standards. Be explicit with what you want from each element and how and when you will monitor it. Make it clear that this is not an option and that failing to meet the standards will result in formal warnings, and eventual dismissal. This might not be necessary because this process frequently leads to either the individual starting to deliver or their deciding they would rather leave of their own accord.

No one wants to spend time firing people, and it makes sense to work with them to correct their performance. At the same time, if they cannot or will not change, you cannot afford to carry underperformers and so have to take action. The important thing is to give them the opportunity to improve.

The sales leader's checklist

- Remember, underperformers cost you both directly and indirectly.

- Not addressing the problem can cause you to lose the respect of other team members, and also lead to others thinking it is acceptable to slacken off.

- Use the sales process and your planning and monitoring systems to act early rather than wait until the actual sales results are behind.

- Always start with a conversation to explore the reasons and ask whether it is a 'can't do' or 'won't do' situation.

- Take the appropriate action depending on the response. Develop or discipline?

- Support and monitor where needed and give encouragement and feedback on improvements. You want to generate even more of the positive behaviour.

- Accept that you cannot change all underperformers and might still have to part company with some of them.

Conclusion – pulling it all together

It is not essential to be a born sales person. In fact, I would debate whether the traditional image of the 'born salesman' is appropriate for professional selling in the 21st century. There are some exceptions in certain sales markets and in different countries who are successful. However, the large majority of successful sales people across most markets have been made through their own determination and development. The bad news: there is not a magic formula which leads to sales success. The good news is that a number of principles and steps will help you to develop into a successful seller if you follow them. Most people can acquire, and use, the skills needed to sell. The differentiator is in the attitude you bring to the challenge. (Having said all of this, there are a few people who will not find sales a suitable role.) The first three parts of this book provide you with the insights to achieve the fundamentals. You need to contribute the determination to apply and practise them.

A large part of your success in sales will come from your willingness to invest time and energy into the various aspects of planning and preparation. This will provide you with the foundation to approach your potential and actual customers with more confidence and to appear more professional to them. The interpersonal and selling skills are important, but they are even more useful if the groundwork has been done. Having them without the preparation does not lead to better results. To convince of value and influence people to buy requires the ability to develop trust, establish what is important to the customer and then show how you can provide it. This can be achieved if you follow the flow of the steps covered in the book. It helps to know how to get commitment and handle barriers, although they are not as high on the skills priority list as relationship building, listening and questioning.

The other factor for sales success is the quality and skills of sales management and leadership being provided. In my experience, the biggest problem for many sales people and sales functions lies in poor sales management. This occurs for various reasons, ranging from poor promotion choices, lack of clarity about the role or lack of skills and knowledge about what the job really involves. My belief is that managers spend too much time focusing on the actual sales results, which may seem strange because they are ultimately responsible for these. However, they do not pay attention to the way results are achieved or how this is done and by whom. The book covers the elements you need to consider and to be able to do. Work on these to develop your competencies and you will achieve better results.

Recognise the need to have a clear sales direction and establish your structure to deliver it. Have the systems in place to ensure that the planning and reporting gives you timely information to monitor and control the right things. Give your sales people the right support and encouragement through offering effective leadership and you are more likely to get results than just operating from behind your desk. Sales management is challenging and is a highly visible role because of the importance of the results to your organisation. Approach it in a balanced way and you can get your costly resource (your sales people) to provide a good return on investment.

Selling and sales management is a great area to work in. The roles will always be challenging and rarely boring. They offer scope for variety, learning and self-development and are needed in virtually every business or professional firm.

Index

Deliver results with this bestselling series

9780273757092

9780273750338

9780273785866

9780273776703

9780273792918

Each book focuses on the key issues and challenges in that area, and breaks each challenge down into sections: understanding the issue, key actions to take, measures of success, pitfalls to watch out for.